D0291279

THE
GREEN
LADY
BOOK II

by

Lisa Picard

Me 'n My Dog
Publishers

ME 'N MY DOG PUBLISHERS

Published by
Me 'n My Dog Publishers
PO Box 2100, Knysna, 6570, South Africa

First published in both e-book and paperback formats
by Me 'n My Dog Publishers, 2015

Printed by Lightning Source

The Green Lady
Copyright © Lisa Picard, 2015
All rights reserved
The moral right of the author has been asserted

Licence Notes

This book is sold subject to the condition that it shall not, by
way of trade or otherwise, be lent, resold, hired out, or
otherwise circulated without the publisher's prior consent in
any form of binding or cover other than that in which it is
published and without a similar condition, including this
condition, being imposed upon the subsequent purchaser.

ISBN: 978-0-620-71655-0

CONTENTS

CONTENTS

DISCLAIMER

This book is set in South Africa's Garden Route and,

specifically, in the town of Knysna, and therefore many of

the places mentioned in the book really do exist.

However, the characters and the stories are purely

fictional and do not depict any actual person or event.

Any resemblance to persons, either living or dead, is

purely coincidental.

PROLOGUE

On a chilly, wet winter's day I arrived in the coastal holiday town of Knysna, South Africa. Piled high in the back of a small pick-up truck that I had loaned from a long-suffering friend, resided all of my worldly possessions. Being a Saturday afternoon, the small town's main road was virtually deserted. Driving past closed shop fronts with darkened windows, I suddenly found my heart filled with misgiving, recalling the vibrant, busy highways of Cape Town, which I had so recently departed. I wondered whether I was cut out for the life in a quiet town that had none of the distractions I was so accustomed to enjoying as a city dweller. There wasn't even a movie house in this one-horse town, for goodness sake! And definitely no sign of stylish coffee shops, award-winning restaurants or glitzy clubs. But there was no turning back now, as my bridges were well-and-truly burnt, I mused, easing the truck into the parking area of the modest apartment building in which I would be living for the foreseeable future. At least there was plenty of available parking; something which no city dweller will ever take for granted.

A sweaty hour later and the pick-up was emptied of my meagre belongings, the bulk of which now resided in the middle of my sitting room inside of a pathetic pile of soggy cardboard boxes. Hanging up my dripping raincoat in the shower, its mouldy, drooping curtain adorned with seventies-style brown and mustard swirls, I was finding it increasingly difficult to keep my spirits up. What on earth had I been thinking to resign from my lucrative job as a journalist at a top Cape Town daily newspaper and move out of my comfortable, stylish house into this tiny, miserable, flea-ridden apartment?

Mentally giving myself a shake and yanking myself back from the temptation of diving head-first into a lengthy wallow in a mire of self-pity, I reminded myself that this had been my own choice. I had willingly given up my career and my city life. For better or for worse, some part of me had decided that this was to be my dream for the future. There was nothing to do now but to make the most of it.

Grabbing a beer from the cooler box on the floor, I threw myself down onto a pile of cushions on the futon, which would have to fulfil the dual function of a bed and a couch in my new Spartan living quarters. Taking a long, cool swig, I mentally reviewed the events that had resulted in my current situation.

Ten months earlier, my long-term girlfriend, Clare, had left me, due to our irreconcilable visions for our shared future. Hers had included marriage and children and mine... well in retrospect I was unsure of exactly what I had wanted at the time. My previously cherished position as a highly-regarded journalist of some fifteen years had no longer been satisfying to me and I had been ready for a change. I just hadn't known exactly what that change would entail.

Then, a series of chance encounters led to my taking a six-month sabbatical in Knysna, during which time I collected stories of super-natural and transformative encounters in the forests of the region for a potential book. My time spent in Knysna culminated in a personal encounter with the mysterious Green Lady, guardian of the forest. This encounter proved to be just as transformative for me as it had been for my interviewees. Upon my return to Cape Town, I had resigned from my job and had set about packing up my life to permanently move back to Knysna, hopefully for good. The plan was to support myself working as a free-lance journalist; inevitably at a fraction of the salary I had previously earned. But my real work would be to finalise the writing of my first book, to get it published and to eventually begin work on the sequel.

Returning from my little trip down memory lane, I clicked my tongue in self-recrimination. My plans now appeared hopelessly optimistic and over-ambitious. What did I know about writing and publishing a book? I'd never published anything longer than a newspaper article before! And who could possibly be interested in the off-the-wall topic I had chosen? Self-pity's siren song beckoned me once again.

Pushing myself up from my prone position and staggering to my feet, clutching my aching back, I lobbed my empty beer can at the wall in disgust. I knew that I would get nothing done in my current mood and so I decided to take myself off to the local pub. I hoped that a few drinks, a basket of deep-fried bits of something or another, and possibly some congenial company would assist me in lifting myself out of my funk.

In the pub I fortuitously encountered Ken Brady, a marine biologist working in Knysna on his PhD project on seahorses, whose story I had included in my first book. By the time we had downed a few beers each, gotten greased-up on pub-grub and bonded over the rugby teams we supported, I was feeling considerably more positive about my situation. I returned to my apartment to start unpacking my few belongings in an attempt to create a slightly less chaotic environment, hopefully more conducive to creativity.

The following morning I awoke, bathed in a brilliant beam of glittering sunlight, with a feeling of excitement in my belly. My blues of the previous day had completely disappeared. I'd made it! Here I was in Knysna, about to commence my new life in which I would follow my heart towards expressing myself as grandly as I could. After a quick breakfast of cereal, I gathered up the flattened cardboard boxes, which I took to the recycling depot, and then bought a prepared sandwich and a few granola bars and got into the truck to drive up the mountain to one of my favourite forest hikes. After all, I reasoned, it was Sunday and I deserved to have at least some time off to recover from my move.

My spirits lifted even further as I stepped out onto the trail. The forest was exquisitely cool and fragrant after the rain, with droplets sparkling on each newly-washed, intensely bright-green leaf. My nostrils welcomed as an old friend the aromas of humus-rich, moist, fertile soil. I found myself humming a jaunty little tune as I stretched my pace, breathing deeply of the healing energies of this most lovely of places.

Within a couple of hours I had reached the massive ancient Yellowwood tree amongst whose roots I had sheltered during my dream-like encounter with the mysterious Knysna elephants earlier that year. Placing my raincoat on the ground to protect my clothing from the damp forest floor, I settled down amongst the roots and enjoyed my picnic. Afterwards, I simply sat basking in the atmosphere of the place. I remembered what the Green Lady had told me about opening my heart and allowing myself to feel love and gratitude toward the forest, and so this is exactly what I did. As I did so, I felt a glow begin to spread from my chest and gradually I remembered exactly why I had decided to uproot my entire life and move to Knysna. Once more I began to feel excited, energised and deeply grateful to be there. The blues of the previous day were by now totally dispelled and I luxuriated in my joyful mood.

Within a few minutes, the light illuminating the pale-green leaves began to deepen to a rich, golden hue. The varied colours and textures of the trees and plants, moss, fungi and lichen began to intensify and I became acutely aware of the magnificent density of life surrounding me... enveloping me. The crickets, frogs and songbirds, the rustling of the undergrowth as small creatures visited this magical place and the chattering of the canopy above as the breeze gently caressed the leaves, all contributed to a delightful, harmonious symphony of vivid life.

The forest held its breath in an extended moment of anticipation. Someone was coming...

And then, suddenly, there she was, gliding across the forest floor towards me, her hands outstretched in welcome, her beautiful face glowing with gentle, green light and her eyes twinkling in a heart-warming smile.

"*Peter, you have returned home at last,*" she said, softly touching my arm with her cool fingertips. I was suffused with intense joy as I realised that her words were true and that I had, indeed, returned to my spiritual and emotional home. I scrambled to my feet with a delightful sense of anticipation. Something wonderful was about to happen!

"*I didn't know that I was coming home. I've only just realised that... this very minute, as you said the words,*" I babbled, feeling overwhelmed with happiness.

"*Peter, you have just begun to follow your heart, to trust in your own authority and in your own knowing, rather than seeking affirmation and direction from outside of yourself. This is the very first step on your journey towards finding and expressing your most authentic self. And you are rightly feeling suffused with joy, because this is simply the most joy-filled journey you will ever undertake! This is the journey to self."*

The Green Lady gracefully sank down onto a moss-covered log and indicated that I too should sit. Then she said, *"Peter, I have been following your progress with great interest and I know that your first book will be enjoyed, and indeed, cherished, by many. But, more importantly, you have contributed towards an increase in consciousness and in love by writing it, even if no-one were ever to read it.*

Now, I know that there is still some work to be done in finalising the book and in making it available for people to purchase and, of course, this work must progress. But, at the same time, you need to start getting into the right frame of mind to write your next book."

"My next book? But... but, I have no plans at the moment to do such a thing. I'm feeling completely intimidated by the huge amount of work required to finish the first book! And, besides, I have absolutely no ideas or inspiration for another book at this time. I'm still trying to come to terms with the massive changes in my life. It's simply too much!" I expostulated, suddenly feeling overwhelmed.

The Green Lady leaned over and placed her hand on my chest, over my heart, and the anxiety left me, to be replaced by a feeling of calm centeredness.

"Peter, it's natural to feel a bit afraid of all this change. But that should not stop you from doing what your heart calls you to do. Your next book is waiting in the wings and, as for inspiration...that's what I'm here for!" A bright, tinkling little laugh that both opened and warmed my heart trilled from her lips.

"Your first book shared the stories of people who had encountered me in the forests of this area. In your next book I will be the one telling the stories. These stories will provide your readers with some insight as to who I am, what is important to me, how I became the Green Lady and what exactly that means," she said.

"Oh, but I would absolutely love to write those stories," I gasped with excitement. "In fact, I can't think of any other stories that I would rather write at this point!"

"And that, my dear friend, is a sure sign that you are on your path; that you are starting to express your most authentic self," she smiled. "Follow the joy, follow the excitement, follow the fascination and the curiosity and they will always lead you to ever greater and greater expressions of self. For now, it will be the writing of The Green Lady, Book II, but, in future, who knows where your joy will lead you!

But let's stay focused for now on the next step. So, what I propose is this: you will come to this place in the forest once a week, on a Sunday afternoon, and we will spend an hour or two together. I will tell you the stories of many experiences I have had and how these experiences have led to my becoming the being you see before you. These will be thrilling stories of seekers and soldiers, of priests and shamans, of aliens and of ordinary human beings. Stories of adventure and discovery but, ultimately, the story of ever-deepening understanding, love and appreciation of the self.

In short, Peter, it is the story of Life discovering itself. And, in the receiving and the writing of my story, you will find yourself on your own journey of discovery of your most magnificent and most authentic self. You will be writing your own story too."

"But, this sounds simply wonderful," I gasped, "I can't wait to begin!"

"Then, I will next see you here in a week's time," she smiled as she stood up, raised her hand in greeting and then drifted away amongst the trees.

I sat for several minutes longer, relishing the excitement of the anticipation of what lay ahead. My new life truly was about to begin...

CHAPTER 1:
BETRAYAL OF THE OTHER

And so it was that I found myself in the forest clearing a week later, anxiously awaiting the appearance of the Green Lady. What if she decided not to turn up after all? With some surprise, I realised that I had my heart set upon writing the new book after all, which was rather strange, considering my reticence of the previous week. Apparently my beautiful green muse had truly inspired me to get on with it.

It had been a busy week; one in which I had written two bread-and-butter articles for local newspapers, had followed up several leads for stories and had made contact with numerous potential sources of future business. In the absence of a regular salary cheque, I needed to make sure that I wouldn't starve whilst I was writing my next book. I had also spent several hours every evening polishing the manuscript of my first book and doing initial research into potential publishers.

As I huddled up amongst the roots of the massive Yellowwood tree, I realised that I was actually rather exhausted after my first week in Knysna and so I allowed my head to drop back against the tree trunk and closed my eyes, relishing the soothing forest sounds and aromas.

"*Already sleeping on the job, I see,*" a gently mocking voice disturbed my slumber and I jumped to my feet, finding myself face-to-face with my green muse.

"*No... not at all... Just meditating and mentally preparing myself to start writing your story,*" I grinned, abashed to be discovered at such a disadvantage, but relieved that she had decided to appear after all. With a graceful wave of her hand, the Green Lady indicated that I should sit down again and she took up position on the moss-covered log where she had sat the previous week. I removed my notebook and pen from my small daypack and made myself comfortable as small, multi-coloured bubbles of excitement fizzed up my spine and popped in my brain. This was it! I was finally going to find out more about the mysterious Green Lady of the forest. And she had picked <u>me</u> to tell her story!

The Green Lady smiled, and I knew that she was completely aware of the thoughts chasing each other and playing hopscotch through my mind. She waited for several minutes, giving me time to compose myself, before saying, "*So, Peter, let's start with a story about betrayal. Betrayal of the worst possible kind. Betrayal of the unity of family and of the community.*"

"*Is this story about you? About where you originated?*" I asked, my inner-journalist needing to place the story in context. "*And is it a true story?*"

"*It seems we will be beginning with a philosophical discussion,*" she smiled. "*Peter, whether any story is true or not actually depends upon your perspective. All stories are true from some perspectives and, equally, all stories are untrue from other perspectives. All self-aware beings fictionalise their experiences and, indeed, their lives. We create stories that make sense of what we have experienced and that allow* us to find meaning and value that will form the foundations for future stories we will tell ourselves about ourselves. This is how we progress in life, creating our reality as we go, story-by-story. There is no ultimately, objectively, true story; all stories are subjective."

"But, wait just a minute there," I objected. "Of course there is an objective reality. Something is either true or false, surely? Sure, I can understand that we create subjective stories to explain our experiences to ourselves in our minds, but there must be one, absolute, ultimate, objective truth about everything. This is what my career as a journalist has been all about - finding the truth!"

"And this is exactly the mistake most people make; believing that there is only one truth and that they are the only ones who know what that truth is! Peter, there is no objective truth. All truth is subjective and a matter of your unique perspective.

At any given moment, you are being bombarded with millions of pieces of information about your world, and your physical senses will only pick up a fraction of a percentage of the information available to you. If you picked up all the available information, your brain would probably explode!

And do you know what the filter is that will allow you to retain some information and discard other information, without even being aware of doing so? It is your beliefs, Peter. Your thoughts about yourself and your world will determine what you perceive in the world. Your perception is a function of your perspective, which, in turn, is the result of your thoughts. This means that you will only ever observe in your reality that which supports the thoughts and beliefs you already have about the world.

You truly don't see the world as it is, but rather, you see the world the way <u>you</u> are!"

"But... but surely we must be able to objectively observe what happens in our world? I mean, for example, scientific instruments can very accurately record data about physical processes. Surely those measurements aren't subjective?"

"Scientific instruments can only record what they are designed to record. They can only measure what you humans believe is there to be measured. And they are also limited by the skill and knowledge of their designers and the technology available at any given time.

And it's not only about recording the information with instruments or with your senses. It's also about the interpretation of the information, which happens in the mind. In fact, you don't see or hear or smell through your eyes and ears and nose; you actually see and hear and smell inside your brain and you interpret these inputs in your mind. You are, in fact, experiencing your entire reality inside your own mind. Reality is not 'out there', but rather, 'in here'," the Green Lady tapped her forehead to illustrate her point.

"OK... I've encountered these kinds of ideas before; like in the story of the three blind men and the elephant. To the man holding the tail, the elephant is a piece of rope; to the man feeling the ear, the elephant is a piece of leather and to the man holding onto the leg, the elephant is a tree-trunk. And to the flea on the elephant's back, the elephant is the entire universe. But the objective truth is that the elephant is a massive, land-based mammal, living on planet Earth!"

"To some, Peter, an elephant would be viewed as an integral part of a complex eco-system; to others the elephant would be a food source; on a molecular level the elephant is a

complex system of inter-related biochemical processes; on the sub-atomic level, the elephant is composed of particles, popping in-and-out of existence in an unimaginably vast field of space and, on the level of energy, the elephant is a standing wave pattern in the zero-point energy field. All of these ideas about the elephant are true from one perspective, and, equally, untrue from another. So, what is the elephant actually, Peter? Do you see that there is no objective truth about the elephant that is eternally valid from all perspectives for all time?"

I was silent for a moment as my mind stretched to accommodate this new thought. Then a further objection arose, "Uh, OK, I do get that. But then... this seems to undermine all certainty we might find in our world; in our experiences. Everything starts to feel rather ambiguous and rather frightening!"

"And the death of certainty is the birth of magic, Peter! The magic of finding your own authentic truth about yourself and about the reality you inhabit, from your own, unique perspective. And this is the process that will lead you home. But we will be covering all this in greater depth during the next few weeks. For now, just accept that it's pointless asking whether a story is true or not.

The better question to ask is this: is it a useful story? And, in that case, I can unambiguously state that, yes, the story I will be telling you today will be a very useful story, as it will give you and your readers a glimpse into how I became the Green Lady, guardian of the forest."

"But, is it a story about a past-life of yours?" I asked, struggling to understand her.

"There are no such things as past-lives, Peter," she smiled.

"Oh... So, <u>this</u> is it then? So there's nothing else besides this life, here now? But, what were you before you became the Green Lady then? I'm totally confused!" I rubbed my eyes, feeling completely out of my depth.

She smiled at me and said, *"Peter, I have had many, many lives and many diverse experiences, as have you, and as have all of your readers. They are just not past-lives, as most people think. Time does not exist outside of this unique, time-bound reality that you currently inhabit - it is all NOW. Which means that there are many lives... and that they are all happening now.*

I can illustrate this point by using the ancient Buddhist metaphor of Indra's jewelled web. It is said that in the abode of the Goddess Indra, there is a wondrous net that stretches into infinity in every single direction. At each node of the net there is a multi-faceted, precious jewel and, since the nodes are infinite, the jewels are infinite too. In each individual jewel, the infinity of all other jewels are reflected and these reflections, in turn, reflect all other jewels and so on... into infinity. When any jewel in the net is touched, all other jewels are affected, which tells us about the inter-connectivity and inter-dependence of all things.

The metaphor of Indra's net originated in the third century Mahayana School, but in more modern times the metaphor of a hologram has been used to indicate that each point is a reflection of every other point.

As you know, a hologram is a three-dimensional image of an object, which is produced by recording on photographic film the interference patterns formed by a split laser beam. These patterns are then illuminated to produce the three-dimensional image with which you will be familiar.

Now, you know that if you were to tear a normal photograph into pieces, you would end up with image confetti; each piece representing only a part of the whole image. However, if you were to break a hologram into pieces, each piece would contain the entire image, only from a slightly different perspective. So, you can see that the hologram is indeed a useful modern analogy for Indra's web.

Now, using again the ancient metaphor of Indra's net, you can see the different lives of a spirit being as represented by the jewels in the net. Each life reflects all the other lives and each life is affected by all the other lives too. This means that a change made in one life will change the other lives as well. All is inter-connected. So, a change that you make in your life here, in this moment of now, ripples out and affects all other lives in the same moment of now. This is such a wonderful thought because it means that everything that you do has infinite consequences. Each thought, word and deed; every intent, can make a massive difference in all of your lives; in fact, in the lives of all other beings."

"*I actually find that thought completely and utterly terrifying!*" I exclaimed, as the impact of what she had just said hit me.

"*Well, it means that you need to become very conscious of what you are creating with your thoughts. And that, until you do, you will continue to experience a random mix of what you might perceive to be good and bad things.*

But, before we get carried away with any further theories, let's just agree that I will be telling you a series of stories that will provide some context for understanding how I became the Green Lady, what my reasons for being the Green Lady are and what my purpose is here on Earth?"

"*I can agree to that,*" I said, happier now that things were moving in a more practical, down-to-earth direction.

"*So, as I mentioned before, this first story is about betrayal...*"

And, with that, the Green Lady began to tell a wondrous tale, both strange and intriguing. She spoke in words of English and yet, as she spoke, images appeared in my mind's-eye allowing me to clearly see what she related. Here is the story she told - the story of the betrayal of the One.

The Council had once more arisen from within the One and had gathered in the place of debating to deal with the threat. The decision the Council would have to take on behalf of the One, in that extended moment, weighed heavily on their collective mind. In all of the Council moments in which the thought-form that called itself Sera had participated, since the first moment of its arising, it had never before felt this level of collective anxiety, dread and fear. These were completely new and unwelcome thoughts.

But... there was something else besides. Something which the thought-form, Sera, alone was carrying in this moment of decision. A terrifying, exhilarating, completely unprecedented secret. A secret which was to tear apart the unity of the One... forever.

All parts of the One were connected on every level and had no knowledge of individuality, such as the beings occupying our reality would understand it. Parts of the One arose, as temporary thought-forms, to fulfil various functions on behalf of the All; for a moment, or for a series of moments and then, once again, coalesced back into the One. And all thought, all knowledge and all outcomes of activity gained by any thought-form were immediately available, in the moment, to the One. The One's greatest strength was its unity. Complete belonging, complete connection, complete Oneness. This current moment, however, was to prove that the greatest strength of the One was also its greatest weakness.

Several moments before this one, something strange and new had emerged. A thought-form had arisen to assist in the Council decision to expand the One into a new dimension. This dimension would allow for much heretofore unprecedented growth and self-knowledge. As the One strove to understand Itself and its origin, it began to ask the question, "*What am I?*" And, in order to answer this question, the One began creating new thought-forms from within Itself to expand into all possible directions that could be thought of, in order to seek answers. These thought-forms expanded and explored and made the new knowledge, thus gained, available to the One, which grew ever more in self-awareness and self-knowledge. Some of these expanding thought-forms arose for only a moment, and some arose for many sequential moments to explore ever further and further reaches of what was.

One of these thought-forms, which had explored for many, many sequential moments, for the first moment ever, began to become self-aware; it became aware of itself as an individual. This thought-form became aware that it could create thoughts of its own and that, most importantly, it could shield these thoughts from the rest of the One. And, within the shielded part of its mind, this thought-form named itself Sera.

Sera discovered that, in a tiny part of its mind-space, thoughts could reside that were not available to the One, unless Sera chose to make them so. It became aware of itself as unique and special and different; as more than simply part of the One. And, in the deep, secret recesses of its own mind, that thought-form that called itself Sera began to resist the idea of simply coalescing back into the One when the function of investigating this new dimension had been fulfilled. Sera became aware of its otherness and, for the first time, individual ego had arisen. This was both magnificent and was also to prove deadly to the integrity of the One.

Sera, and the other thought-forms that had arisen to be in the place of debating and deciding, began the process of the Council. Firstly, they reviewed within their collective mind what had occurred in the moments leading up to this moment:

Within the new dimension that Sera had been exploring, it had encountered an Other that was not part of the One. This was a monumental discovery, as all expansions to this point had been only within the mind of the One. But this Other was outside of the mind of the One. It was not available or accessible to the mind of the One and the One found that it could not know the thoughts of this Other.

Sera had called out to this Other from the mind of the One. "*What are you?*" Sera called, "*How do you come to be here in this moment? How may we know you?*"

The Other did not respond as a thought arising in the mind of the One. The response arrived in a form that the One had never before encountered: an image of violence and aggression, not in the thoughts of Sera, but rather projected somehow in a kind of expression that had never been encountered by the One before. This projection showed the utter destruction of the One; the breaking apart of the connection, the drifting, the never-before encountered concept of aloneness.

Then the Other demonstrated to the One that there were indeed many other ones. The One was not the only one!

This was an incredible thought within the mind of the One, but stranger and even more terrible thoughts were to arise for the first time in the moments that followed.

The Other selected one of these other ones and demonstrated that it was capable of carrying out its threat. Projected onto the substance of this dimension, the Other showed the complete destruction of another one. The mind of Sera struggled to comprehend what it was being shown. This Other could indeed annihilate an other one if it chose to do so. It was possible for the One to exist no more if this Other chose to carry out its threat! The mind of the One was cast into turmoil and the thought called fear arose for the very first time.

Then the Other showed the One yet another projection. In this projection, the circle of the Council was disbanded. The thought-forms in the Council relinquished their right to decide for the One. They simply allowed the Other to enter the circle; to enter the One. And this was an image of peace and love and unity. The Other entered the One and promoted its growth and expansion and self-knowledge. The Other offered everything that the One had always strived towards. But the price was high. The price was the surrendering of the inviolability of the One. The price was permitting the Other into the sanctity of the One.

Then the Other showed Sera a projection of a few moments of now in which the One had an opportunity to decide. And, for the first time, the thought called urgency arose within the One. There was not an infinity of moments in which to decide. A decision would need to be made, in this moment, Now!

Within the secret part of Sera's mind, it felt terror. The threat was not just to the One as a whole; more importantly, the threat was to Sera as an individual! Sera knew that it was not willing to allow itself, as an individual, to be annihilated. It had had but a few precious moments of being self-aware. It wanted so many more moments. In fact, Sera wanted the moment of its individual existence to never cease. And, in that moment, Sera knew that it would use all of its newfound abilities to ensure that it would continue to exist, for all future moments. Sera would fight for its own survival, even at the expense of the One!

And so Sera spoke to the Other, from within the secret part of itself, so as to ensure that the One would not be aware of the conversation. And Sera created a thought-form that it projected to the Other: "*I am Sera. I am unique and special and I can speak to you on my own. I am on the Council and I have complete knowledge of the ways of the One. I can sway the Council to accept your proposal. But, in return, I want you to give me assurance that I will survive as an individual. I want knowledge of what is outside of the One. I want to see and experience all that is outside of me.*"

The Other promised Sera all that it asked, saying, "*You are indeed special and different. You are the next step in the evolution of the One and you shall be held up in highest regard and esteem by us. You shall be given knowledge and abilities far beyond what you can create in your mind in this moment. Influence the Council to decide in our favour and you shall have it all. You shall continue to exist for all moments to come.*"

As the Council reviewed the thoughts that Sera had made available from the interaction with the Other, Sera carefully screened the thoughts of its private interaction with the Other from the rest of the One.

The first thought that arose in the Council was that the One should not comply with the demands of the Other. *"Our strength is our unity; our strength is our connection. If we break that connection we are completely vulnerable. This Other is powerful beyond anything we have ever thought. How do we know it will do as it promises? How do we know that it won't just destroy us anyway once we have dissolved the circle of the Council?"*

But Sera used its newfound ability to think unique thoughts that were separate from the thoughts of the rest of the One: *"This Other offers the One so much more than we could ever have thought on our own. Our deepest desire is to know ourselves; to understand what we are and where we have originated. This Other promises us so much scope to explore that question. We are offered expansion of the One, way beyond even our most magnificent thoughts in any moment before. We should comply."*

Then other thought-forms arose, *"But perhaps we should remain exactly as we have always been in every other moment of now? We have, until the moment of meeting this Other, been peaceful and happy and complete. We didn't know that we were happy because there was no other way to contrast with what we had always experienced. But now we know that we were always happy; now that we have experienced other thoughts of fear and loss. Why change what has always worked?"*

And Sera again responded, allowing the One to access its thoughts, but not all of its thoughts, *"The moment for change has come anyway. If we don't comply, the One will be destroyed and there will be no further expansion in any moments at all. By allowing for change in this moment, the*

One assures its survival and also its expansion in all moments to come."

On-and-on the debate raged. Thought-forms arose and were countered by other thought-forms, which, in turn, were pitted against more complex and sophisticated thought-forms. In the process, the One found itself changing, evolving and rapidly growing in the understanding of its nature. Never before had such a challenge been experienced and never before had such a response been forthcoming. But, by the end of the moment, Sera's thought had prevailed. The Council would dissolve into the One, relinquishing its position as guardian and decision-maker. The final act of the Council would be to open the One to the entrance of the Other.

And so it was decided. And so it was.

And in that final moment, as the Council coalesced into the One for the final time and allowed the Other entrance, the knowledge arose in the mind of the One of the fatal mistake it had made. The Other invaded the One and completely destroyed it from the inside.

Sera's final thoughts as it spun away from the One for the very first time were, *"It was a mistake. The Other needed the One to permit it entry. The projections of the Other were not the truth. The truth is that the unity of the One would always have protected it in every moment. The only way the Other could have destroyed the One was by our co-operation. The Other lied to us. And I have betrayed us!"*

And then there was only aloneness, disconnection and drifting... lost... lonely... in an infinite void.

As the Green Lady's incredible story came to an end, I sat for a long moment, simply staring at her; completely at a loss as to what to think about the story I had just heard. *"But... but that's simply unbelievable!"* I finally expostulated. *"Surely this story can't be true? Do you really expect me to believe that there are beings that occupy such a vastly different reality from ours? It's like science fiction of the worst possible kind! And, if there were such beings, how does that being... what was its name? Sera... how does that being relate to you?"*

The Green Lady smiled her usual calm and serene smile at me and said, *"Remember what I told you before we started, Peter? It's <u>all</u> just a story. Your life and mine - they're just stories that we tell ourselves in order to make sense of our experiences. We all fictionalise our so-called memories. There is no past - just the ever-present moment of now.*

In the case of Sera, this is a story about an experience of mine that will eventually contribute to your making sense of how I came to be who I am, and where I am. So, the question to ask, remember, is whether the story is useful, not whether it is true, because... from a certain perspective everything is true and from another perspective, everything is not true."

"OK, OK, I remember. And I do get that. I guess it's just a stretch for me to keep it in mind when I am confronted with such strange stories!" I sighed.

"I daresay that the story I have just told you is not nearly as difficult to believe as that you are right now sitting here in the forest, sharing philosophical discussion and tales of other lives with a woman made of green light," she giggled. I had to concede that she had a point. Ever since my hike up Table Mountain in Cape Town, during which I had encountered an apparition which had helped to set me on my current life path, my life had been getting progressively stranger and stranger!

"All right, then, I'm prepared to hold lightly to notions of true and false whilst I write down these stories of yours," I said. *"I can see that it's going to be a stretch for me, though! So, what happened to Sera and the remnants of the One, then?"*

"We'll pick up Sera's story again in a few weeks' time, Peter. But first there are many other, inter-connected, stories that I must tell you so that you will finally be able to make sense of it all. So, be patient. All will be revealed in good time!"

"OK, then, what story will you tell me next?"

As I asked the question, I became aware of a frisson of excitement. This was turning out to the best fun I'd had in a long time and, although the story I had just been told was strange, it was certainly original and interesting! I realised that I was really looking forward to seeing how the narrative of the Green Lady would unfold in the weeks to come. I could also see that my mind would have to expand considerably in order to accommodate all the new thoughts and ideas with which I would inevitably be presented.

"You're just going to have to wait until next week to see, Peter!" she said with a smile. *"And I suggest that you arrive an hour earlier next week because it will be a much longer story and we don't want to run out of daylight before we reach a natural pause point."*

With that, the Green Lady rose gracefully to her feet, blew me a kiss and disappeared amongst the trees.

I hiked back out of the forest with a spring in my step. The next few weeks promised to be an amazing journey!

CHAPTER 2:
BETRAYAL OF THE SELF
(PART 1)

The following Sunday I made sure that I arrived at the clearing in the forest more than an hour before my arrival time of the previous week. But, despite that, the Green Lady was already sitting on the moss-covered log waiting for me when I arrived and we immediately set to work recording her next story.

"Peter, last week's story was about betrayal of the unity of family and community. Today I will be telling you a story of a far worse betrayal - the betrayal of the self." With a delicious shiver of anticipation, I settled down amongst the tree roots, my notebook and pen poised to capture today's tale.

She dances... the firelight illuminating her high, round cheekbones, which glisten with perspiration; her taut and lithe, yet voluptuous body twisting and turning in a sensuous rhythm older than time itself. Her shadow leaping and twirling on the windbreak of reeds and grasses. Her feet kicking up sea sand as she spins. The massive sandstone cliffs are silent sentinels to this ancient ritual; the rhythmic boom of the ocean providing the bass to the heart-music only she can hear.

Earth, air, fire, water; the four elements powerfully present in this most sacred of places. The tribe gathered around the fire watches intently as she increases the pace of her dance; their chanting increasing in speed to match her rhythm.

Lemma... my sister! My heart swells with awe and pride. The familiar face of my childhood companion becomes mysterious and unknowable in this fire-lit ritual and my excitement is tinged with the sadness of impending loss.

"Didu, someday it will be you," whispers Nanni, the mother of my mother, and my heart flip-flops in my chest with a mixture of excitement and trepidation.

My sister dances the sacred dance of immortality; the immortality of our tribe. Her dance recalls the ancient stories of our people. Now she dances the story of the growth of our civilisation; her widespread arms and thrown-back head reminding us of the journeys through space and dimensions undertaken by our forebears in the expansion of our tribe. Her fingers and hands begin to weave intricate patterns as she dances our much-valued freedom of personal creative expression.

As I watch my sister's feet slowing now to dance the time of the slavery of our ancestors, I remember my Nanni's husky voice relating this very story to us when we were small children, sitting around the bonfire at night. The story of the Motherland and her peoples, from way beyond the deepest mists of time...

"Draw closer, little ones. Settle down now. Sit very quietly here, in a circle around me... that's right, sit here in front of the fire and let me tell you the story of how our people came to be. It's a story of great courage and exciting adventures. Of distant star systems and alien civilisations. Of war and loss and devastation; and, ultimately, transformation.

A story of being utterly lost, in the darkest depths of forgetting but yet, always with the possibility of finding the way home again."

  In a time, long before recorded time, there was a Great Spirit that wished to explore the nature of its own being. In order to do so, it decided to express itself into a new reality. To lower its energies into ever deeper and deeper densities. To discover what it truly was by gradually, and willingly, entering into a state of forgetfulness. What would it create, the Spirit wondered; what would it become, if it forgot what it truly was?

  The Great Spirit split itself into two original archetypes; the male and the female. Or, the god and the goddess. All other spirit beings that wished to enter into this new reality to participate in this new game would now similarly have to split themselves into these two original archetypes. The male and the female were two perfectly balanced opposites. The male part was called Adamu, and the female part was called Eva. Adamu and Eva were really two sides of the same one being.

  Eva and Adamu started up two separate small civilisations, separated by an ocean, on a distant planet. This was a new game to Eva and Adamu and they were engaged in a friendly competition to see whose civilisation could advance the furthest and the best.

"Wait a minute here! I have some questions."

The Green Lady paused in her narrative and smiled at me, "*Yes Peter, I know that you do. What would you like to ask me?*"

"*Well, I'm not sure I understand what is meant by this spirit being "expressing itself" into a reality. And also, how can a spirit being forget who it is? And, thirdly, is this a weird, alternative version of the creation myth of the Christian Bible?*"

"*A spirit being expressing itself into a reality is a bit like putting a hand into a glove. Although the immortal spirit being remains outside of time, it can clothe a part of itself in the energy density of a specific reality. Each reality is different, and there are different set-up conditions for each reality, which are agreed upon by the beings expressing themselves into that reality. In the case of the reality we are discussing at the moment, the set-up conditions included a split into the male and female archetypes and a gradual forgetting of the true nature of the self. These are, of course, also the prevailing conditions of the reality that we currently inhabit.*"

"*But how can a being forget who and what it is?*"

"*By expressing itself through a construct called the Veil of Forgetting. This is another, rather complex, set-up condition of this reality, which we won't explore in any further depth at the moment, or we might find ourselves becoming completely distracted from the story at hand. However, you can read about this construct in many excellent books covering the topic[1]. That part of the spirit being which is outside of the reality remembers full well what it is; but that part which is*

---

1   There is a very detailed description of the Veil of Forgetting in Book 1 of *The Ascension Papers* by Zingdad. Indeed a whole chapter of that work is dedicated to this very topic. This is well worth the read for the additional insights it offers into why the world is as it is, and why we are as we are when we are here, beyond the Veil.

inside of the reality - the hand inside the glove, as it were - gradually forgets entirely who and what it truly is."

"Do all realities, into which a being can express, have forgetting associated?"

"Not at all! This is a very unusual set-up condition, which leads to unparalleled opportunities for growth and re-creation of self. But it can also be extremely challenging, and beings can lose a part of themselves for a very long time in such a reality."

"You say, 'a part of themselves'. Does this mean that the spirit being outside of time is also expressed in many other realities at the same time?"

"Of course! The spirit being is outside of time, as we discussed previously. All lifetimes and all expressions in all realities are happening in the same moment of now. It is just for the part expressed into this particular reality that the illusion of time, and also the forgetting, is applicable."

"So, what you are saying is that my higher self, the immortal spirit being that I truly am, is outside of time, expressing itself into all of my several, time-bound lifetimes, and also into many other realities, all in the same moment of now?"

The Green Lady's face lit up, "Well done, Peter! You are finally beginning to understand!

And, in answer to your question about the Judeo-Christian creation myth, I would like to remind you of what I have said before: all is story. You and I are spending time together so that I might tell you stories. And all lives are stories. Including yours, and including mine. And all religions too are stories.

Now, if one story seems to bear some resemblance in some of its facets to another story, then that is not strange.

Since all is One, the ultimate story-teller is the same One Great Spirit that resides in the heart of all that is. But all stories will also have differences amongst them too, since each story is inevitably being told from a different perspective. That is their beauty and their value. And so I exhort you again, Peter: with this story, as with all stories, hold lightly to the story whilst you seek its usefulness and its beauty. Release your attachment to needing it to be true. For no story that has ever been told has been irrefutably true from all perspectives. Now, may we continue?

"OK, I'm sure I'll have plenty more questions later on. But let's carry on for now."

Time passed upon that distant planet and the civilisations of Eva and Adamu advanced, in equal but opposite ways. And then the great attack came.

Both civilisations were attacked by a very warlike, advanced and aggressive race which came from a distant star system. Eva and Adamu's fledgling civilisations did not possess the kind of technology that their attackers had and most of these two young civilisations were completely wiped out in their attackers' first surprise onslaught. It was their enemy's intention to completely obliterate both civilisations. But they were totally unaware that there were spiritual masters within both civilisations upon the planet. These were beings that had ascended their consciousness to such a high level that they were able to create and hold a light-body into which they could accept a number of others who were less spiritually advanced. And, to the attackers' great surprise, they noticed what looked like minute suns lighting up upon the planet's surface and then darting off into space at speeds beyond anything they had imagined possible.

And so the attack failed. Not only were these two civilisations not destroyed, but indeed, as a result of this attack, they came to be seeded throughout the galaxy, as the descendants of these remaining individuals of both civilisations were to find temporary homes on many different planets at many different dimensions over the next few millennia.

As Eva and Adamu evolved their civilisations further, as they moved deeper and deeper into the game, their energies were stepped down, deeper and deeper into forgetfulness, just as had been planned from the beginning. The ultimate plan was always that their two civilizations would eventually be able to find balance and completeness in each other. Out of the deepest forgetfulness, the two civilisations would eventually find unity, and so leave the game. But this plan would only finally come to fruition in a very far distant future; a future that has not yet come to pass from the perspective of the beings currently inhabiting planet Earth.

As the two civilisations developed at ever deeper and deeper density levels, Eva and Adamu eventually found the perfect place for their respective peoples. It was our current solar system. Eva took Planet Earth as the home for her people and Adamu took Mars. They were, at the time, twin planets and remarkably alike.

Deep in density, these civilizations were now quite unaware of each other and of the greater picture. Adamu's civilization on Mars developed along what might be called masculine lines. This civilisation was called the Atlanteans. And their land was called Atlantis.

"Whoa, whoa, whoa! Are you telling me that the myth of Atlantis is real? And that Atlantis was on Mars! Oh, wait... I know what you're going to say. This is just a story, right? Hold lightly... OK, I'm sorry I interrupted. Please continue."

Whilst the Atlantians were evolving their civilisation on Mars, Eva's tribe was establishing itself on Earth as the Lemurians. The differences between the two civilizations were quite profound. The Atlanteans were analytical, logical, competitive, aggressive and dominating. They were in a constant state of internal strife and war. This constant strife allowed them to grow strong, wily and adaptable and it also fostered the development of ever more powerful technology.

By contrast, the Lemurians were intuitive, spiritual, emotional, co-operative, peace-loving and submissive. Their high levels of empathy meant that they really did feel the other to be as self and knew that to harm the other or the planet was to harm the self. They were vegetarians, as the animals were seen to be brothers and sisters to themselves. And they recognised the sentience of everything, including the planet itself.

In fact, the Lemurians' aversion to conflict was almost pathological. They were not willing or able to find aggression within themselves; not even to defend themselves. This certainly inhibited their advancement and caused them to languish in terms of technological inventions. But they were still a most marvellous and beautiful civilization. Their ability to express themselves artistically was unrivalled. The depth of empathy that existed amongst individuals was truly advanced. They were all about harmony and love.

The Atlanteans, by contrast, were in constant competition with each other. They used their mighty brains to find ever more powerful ways of dominating each other. Technology flowered at a fantastic pace, including destructive technologies. And so it came to be that the Atlanteans developed nuclear weaponry. They were hot-headed and they used this technology against each other; the effect being that their home planet was pretty much wiped clean of life. The areas that were bombed were utterly stripped of their capacity to support life. And the remaining planet became enshrouded in a toxic cloud. It was a matter of a few short years before all higher life on Mars (then known as Atlantis) came to an end.

However, the Atlanteans had, by then, developed space-flight technology and a small number of them escaped to a landmass on their neighbouring planet, Earth. They called the new land, Atlantis, in memory of the old and they quite quickly built it to resemble the old one on Mars. They signed declarations about how they would work together in future and never again engage in self-destructive warfare. A code was enacted to disallow the development of armies and weapons of mass destruction to be used against their own people. They didn't want to ever repeat the actions that had led to the destruction of their original home planet.

And so the Atlantean civilisation, once again, grew and prospered. After some time, they inevitably met up with the Lemurians.

The Lemurians had made a practice of living underground. As with all things, they believed that the rock was sentient and that tunnelling was an act of intimacy with the Earth. They believed that Mother Earth spoke to them and told them where to tunnel. Their vast, organically-shaped caverns and tunnel systems provided them with connectivity and communication without risking interaction with the wild animals of their home planet, Earth. This is how they remained safe without ever engaging in violence.

But the invading Atlanteans were a different proposition altogether. They were not wild animals, nor were they the primitive ape-men that also roamed the Earth at that time. They were highly advanced and highly technological and they were actively reconnoitring their new home planet for mineral ores so that they could produce metals and thereby further advance their technologies and their civilisation. Their deep-scanning devices quickly picked up tunnel anomalies, which were traced, and the entrances were found. Armed reconnaissance teams were sent in to explore the tunnels and, inevitably, the Atlanteans met up with the Lemurians for the first time.

There could not possibly have been a greater disaster for the Lemurians. The Atlanteans blasted open their tunnels, marched right in and hauled them out.

Meeting up with the Lemurians for the first time, the Atlanteans immediately decided that their fellow sentient hominid inhabitants of Earth were considerably inferior specimens. Atlanteans were tall and muscular, with blonde hair and blue or blue-green eyes, whereas the Lemurians were generally far smaller, with a slighter stature and dark, curly hair and brown eyes.

There was an initial attempt at communication, but there was such a profound disconnect in their ways that the two civilisations utterly failed to effectively communicate. The

Atlanteans decided that the Lemurians were far too primitive and stupid to understand their superior language and culture and that they had nothing of any value to offer to the Atlantean civilisation, other than their labour. They decided to round the Lemurians up and use them as slaves, which proved to be a complete disaster. The Lemurians were not able to resist the Atlanteans in any way. But their inherent soul-connection with the Earth and with each other was such that they became abominably traumatized by their captivity. They began to die in droves before they could even begin to be trained by the Atlanteans, and the few remaining survivors were eventually set free.

Fast forward many hundreds of years and the two civilizations had reached an uneasy truce. There was limited trade and certain individuals had managed to learn a little of each others' languages and cultures. As a result of acts of sexual aggression by Atlantean men on Lemurian women, there was a growing population of hybrids, who then inter-bred amongst themselves. There were also willing partnerships between Atlantean men and Lemurian women, which resulted in hybrid children being born. Such individuals had a difficult life, as they often found it impossible to live within the Lemurian society, which they found to be apathetic, slow, backward and lacking in drive and ambition. However, they were treated as second-class citizens by the Atlantean society and so they tended to congregate with other hybrids. Thus, whole hybrid neighbourhoods sprung up, which developed their own bastardised language and culture.

But the time of Lemuria was drawing to a close. They had, as a civilization, essentially accomplished what they had come to this reality for. The souls that had incarnated several lifetimes as Lemurians were beginning to move on. The

Lemurian civilization was gradually drawing to a close, whereas the Atlantean civilisation was still on the ascendant.

The remaining Lemurians were still highly artistic and creative, empathic and intuitive. But the Atlanteans saw them as inherently inferior due to the fact that they were not blessed with a great aptitude for the kind of critical reasoning that the Atlanteans prized. Though quite intelligent enough, the Lemurians did not show an inclination towards technology, machinery or mining. And, due in part to genetic factors and also in part to their unwillingness to eat meat and animal products, the Lemurians were also quite slight of build, making them unsuitable for strenuous manual labour. In addition, they were simply unwilling to engage in aggression of any kind and so were unsuitable to be trained as soldiers.

However, the Atlanteans did come to value and prize the Lemurian abilities in the performing arts: singing and dancing, for example. The Lemurians were also known to be wonderful cooks and gardeners. And so the remarkable Lemurian abilities were down-graded to humble serving, gardening and entertainer positions in Atlantean culture.

There were periodic raids by groups of Atlanteans on the Lemurians in order to capture young Lemurians, who were then sold as slaves to work as cooks or entertainers in the homes of the wealthier Atlanteans. In the intervening years, the Atlanteans had learned enough about Lemurian culture and constitution to keep their slaves alive. Officially, this practice was frowned upon, but in the absence of legislation actively prohibiting it, the practice continued and officials turned a blind eye. There was very little the Lemurians could do to stop this practice, other than burrow ever deeper into their caves and tunnels and be constantly vigilant and secretive so as to avoid notice by the roving bands of slavers.

It is at this point in the story that we first meet up with Didu, a young Lemurian girl.

Didu was the second daughter of Era; her older sister being Lemma, an extremely talented young woman who had been selected to train to eventually become an adept in the Naacals, the Lemurian mystery school. Era had been taken captive by the Atlanteans during one of their raids shortly after the birth of Didu and rumour had it that she had died in captivity a few months later. The two girls had been raised by their maternal grandmother, along with four other children, as their grandmother was a trained and designated Lemurian child rearing specialist. Of course, as was the custom in Lemurian society, neither girl knew the identity of her biological father.

During the annual time of coming together, all selected participating Lemurians would meet for the ancient ritual of sacred sexuality; the merging of the energies. The purpose of this ritual was the conception of children, who would be cared for by child rearing specialists and would be the responsibility of the entire community. These sacred rituals were shrouded in mystery and only those participating and the members of the Council knew exactly what occurred there. Anyone who participated took an oath of silence, for which the punishment of breaking was expulsion from the tribe. This was, in effect, a death sentence, as Lemurians would never be able to survive on their own without their tribe. It was a great honour to be selected to participate in the rituals and only the strongest, best and most talented were selected by the Council of Elders.

"Could you stop there, please? I'm very interested in this part of the tale. I've heard stories about ancient civilisations that practised sacred sexuality, for various purposes, even to gain immortality. Was this a similar ritual?"

"Oh yes, Peter, the Lemurians did indeed practice various forms of sacred sexuality. One form was practised to bring forth children, which is what I was describing above.

There was no concept of the nuclear family in the Lemurian society of the time. Children were raised by the community and there was never a sense of "ownership" of, or responsibility for, individual children by a couple, such as you have on Earth now. Lemurians deemed by the Council to be most suited to the bearing and/or raising of children were assigned these roles and the roles of child bearing and child raising were always separated. So, while each mother would usually have an abundance of loving contact with her child, it would not be her responsibility to raise her child. Only the wisest and most patient were trained to be child-rearing specialists. Nanni, Didu's grandmother, was one such specialist. These individuals were held in high regard by the tribe and were deferred to on all matters pertaining to the raising of the young. This meant that they were seen to be the shapers of the future of the tribe. And the clan afforded them every possible resource and support to ensure that they could optimally accomplish their sacred task.

In addition to bringing forth children, another type of sacred sexuality practised by the Lemurians had the aim of allowing the participants to have a personal experience of the Divine. These experiences would ultimately enable the attainment of a form of immortality, not for the individual, but for the civilisation as a whole."

"Oh, this is fascinating! Please would you tell me more?"

"Well, this is only tangentially germane to the story of Didu, but sure, I'll tell you a bit more about it.

The Lemurians incorporated continual touch and sensuality into their everyday lives. They expressed themselves sensually and sexually as a means of strengthening community love and unity. This encouraged the development of very deep and powerful community bonds. The Lemurians were very open sexually and had few taboos. As a people, they were highly empathic, and had no concept of possessiveness or jealousy.

In addition to this everyday sensuality, the Lemurians also practiced sacred sexuality as a high art form. There were all manner of sexual rituals which were taught at various stages of life in which individuals were able to access their own divinity through sexuality, which is what we were discussing earlier. The closest to this that you might have heard of is the concept of tantric sex. But the art practiced by the Lemurians went well beyond this. The consciousness of the participants was elevated to the point of ecstatic union with the divine. This form of sacred sexuality was taught to, and practised by, all adult members of society as an art form and as a religious observance.

However, certain carefully selected and highly trained members of society, the adepts, who lived apart from the rest, were responsible for ancient rituals, shrouded in mystery. These rituals were all about interpreting the will of the Divine, ensuring the well-being of all their people and ultimately, about ascension of the whole of the civilisation. The knowledge and wisdom of these adepts was consulted in all Council decisions affecting the people.

It is actually in large part thanks to the Lemurian practices of sacred sexuality that the civilisation was coming to a close. It was, in fact, ascending. Upon leaving their bodies at death, individuals were finding their consciousness to be of too high a vibration to keep returning. One by one they stopped coming back; stopped re-incarnating. And the civilization shrank. Very shortly, the remaining Lemurians would all depart from this reality, never to return. But we'll hear more about that later.

Now the Atlanteans, on the other hand, had an entirely different interest in sex. They had the same plumbing as the Lemurians, but the incarnating spirit was of different intent. The Atlanteans were not too big on spiritual pursuits. To put it mildly. For the Atlanteans sexuality was far more about domination and competition and pandering to the ego. To get an idea of their style of sexual engagement you should probably picture a randy male-chauvinist from your own era. They wanted to have sex with each other as a culmination of the hunt and chase. Status was gained from "conquering" a particularly desirable "target".

The societal norms that grew out of this approach to sexuality were quite interesting. In a strange way the society became quite sexually repressed. You see, you lost status if you were seen to be "easy". And high status individuals believed that they "owned" the sexuality of their lower-status sexual partners. And if someone tried to woo your partner, it was considered to be a terrible affront. This could quite easily give rise to violent conflict; sometimes even to death.

Parents would vigorously protect the "virtue" of their children so that they remained chaste until a suitably high-status individual came a-calling.

An interesting society. Highly pre-occupied with sex and with winning and maintaining the right partner. But, for all that, they were substantially less interested in the sex act itself. They had no idea of the power and the value of the mysterious, potentially transformative, act of sex.

I'm sure you can imagine that there would have been a very interesting sexual dynamic very early on when these two civilisations encountered each other. The Atlanteans were bemused by the sexual openness of the Lemurians. They experienced Lemurian sexuality with a combination of fascination and repulsion. And, of course, they had no frame of reference for understanding the role of sexuality and sensuality in the Lemurian culture.

But now, our daylight is rapidly running out. I think I'll have to complete this story next week."

CHAPTER 3:
BETRAYAL OF THE SELF
(PART 2)

"*P*eter, last week I began the story of Didu and the history of the Atlanteans and the Lemurians. We spoke about sacred sexuality in Lemurian society and the inherent differences between the Atlantean and Lemurian ways of being. This week I will continue with Didu's story: the story of betrayal."

"I'm ready, and also extremely interested in hearing how this fascinating story unfolds."

"Good. So, let's get started then, shall we? Last week I started telling you the story of Didu and her sister Lemma, who was to dance the initiation rites to be accepted as an adept of the Naacals. Let me start today with how Lemma came to be doing just that."

In Lemurian society, leadership was provided by a Council of Elders: a group of thirteen well-respected men and women who were elected from within the general populace and who served on the Council for a term of five years. The Council was responsible for all decision-making on behalf of their people and were absolutely trusted by the Lemurians to take the very best decisions for the tribe as a whole. The

Council took advice and input on all decisions from the adepts, who lived apart from the rest of the Lemurians in a secret monastery, buried deep within the mountains. The adepts were able to interpret the will of the divine and thereby ensure that all decisions affecting the people were made with the will of the Goddess in mind.

The Council chose a group of the most promising youngsters every year to be trained in the mystery school. Those chosen would, from the age of twelve, receive training in self mastery, advanced meditation, telepathy, empathy and, of course, in the practices of sacred sexuality. They studied the ancient Lemurian texts at the feet of the master teachers, who had themselves previously been trained as adepts. The students learned to hone their intuition to a fine degree. In addition, they extensively studied the history of their people and of their home planet. During the first six years of their training, they would continue to live within the community and attend school for a number of hours every day. But, by the age of eighteen, their initial training would be complete. Those trained in the mystery school would generally take up positions of influence and responsibility within their community, including teaching and also serving on the Council.

One final-year student would be selected every year to be initiated as an adept and, after the initiation ceremony, would leave his or her home and family in order to join the other adepts in the monastery, where they would join in The Great Work, which would eventually result in the ascension of all Lemurians out of this system. None of the general populace knew exactly what that work entailed, but it was rumoured that the adepts had mastered the secrets of personal immortality, in service of tribal immortality. The adepts would work together until they reached a critical mass, which would allow them to assist in the ascension of all the remaining Lemurians on Earth to the next dimension of existence. Certainly, they were able to provide great wisdom and insight into all Council decisions affecting the general populace. And this brings us back now to the story of Didu.

That year, Didu's sister had been selected from amongst all the possible candidates to become an adept. Lemma had shown great promise from a very early age. In a people who were all highly gifted in telepathy and other spiritual talents, Lemma stood out. She had remained top of her class for the entire six years of her training at the school and had been the obvious choice as the selected adept for that year.

Didu herself had just turned twelve and she too had recently been selected to be trained in the mystery school over the next six years. Her schooling would commence in a few week's time. She had a good idea of what to expect, as her sister had been telling Didu about her own lessons for the past six years. Lemma was a gifted teacher and found that she was better able to remember her own lessons if she taught them to Didu. Didu could still hear her sister's voice echoing in her mind, "*Didu, remember that thought always precedes actions. Whenever you wish to alter your reality, you must first change yourself by changing your thoughts. The world is merely a mirror. If you don't like what you see in the mirror, then it makes no sense to try and change the mirror. No, you must change yourself and then the image you see in the mirror will automatically change. Remember, you cannot change others. You can only change yourself.*"

Didu was very proud of her sister for being selected as an adept but also sad about losing her. She knew that becoming an adept was the crowning achievement of Lemma's life to date and that every young person dreamed of achieving this honour. Although Didu knew that Nanni would continue to look after her for the next six years, just as she always had, still her sister leaving would result in a gaping hole in her young life.

Didu also knew that Lemma would have to leave that very evening, directly after the initiation rites were completed. She knew that Lemma would probably never see her family again, unless Didu herself was selected as an adept in six years time and joined her sister at the monastery. It also meant that Lemma would never have the opportunity of being selected to participate in the rituals of sacred sexuality to have a child; would never become a teacher or a Council member or be entrusted with the sacred responsibility of raising children. These were just some of the many sacrifices required of those who were chosen to become adepts.

However, Didu knew that if she worked really hard and was selected as an adept, she would be able to join her sister in the monastery in the mountain and that Lemma would not have aged a day from the way she looked right now.

As Didu sadly contemplated the imminent departure of her sister, she found herself fervently wishing that her best friend, Reyna, could be there by her side, to make the transition a little easier for her. But Reyna had left the clan to go and stay with her Lemurian mother and Atlantean father in one of the hybrid compounds a few months earlier. It was rumoured that Reyna had been employed as a servant in one of the Atlantean monastery schools.

Reyna's mother, Petta, had met her father, Zandar, who was an Atlantean anthropologist studying the Lemurian burial rites, when he had been interviewing several members of her clan. Of course Zandar had studied the Lemurian language in order to effectively carry out his studies. This was quite a feat for an Atlantean, as the Lemurian language was a combination of vocalisations, intonations, inflections and physical and facial expressions. It was extremely subtle, highly nuanced and very difficult for a non-Lemurian to properly master.

Zandar, who was considered to be quiet and introverted and a bit of a gentle soul amongst his Atlantean counterparts, found the Lemurian language easier to master than did most Atlanteans. Despite this, it took him the better part of two years of constant study to do so.

Petta, on the other hand, picked up the rather simpler Atlantean language within a few months. She had always been intelligent and adventurous and was considered to be somewhat wild and uncontrollable by her Lemurian clan members. It was just like her to rebel against her culture by picking an Atlantean mate. However, it had actually been love at first sight, and not at all an attempt at rebellion that had drawn her to Zandar and, despite the censure of their respective families, Petta and Zandar had decided to form a life-bond. They had moved to a hybrid compound within a day's walk of the tunnels in which Petta's family lived.

When Petta gave birth to Reyna, she approached the Lemurian Council to find a suitable person to raise the child, as was the custom. Despite her own choice of life partner, Petta wanted her child to be raised in the gentle and loving Lemurian culture, rather than in the aggressively competitive Atlantean culture. The Council had grave reservations about raising a hybrid child amongst their own, but Didu's grandmother, Nanni, agreed to raise Reyna and so Reyna became Didu's best friend and clan sister.

The two girls were both somewhat different from other girls of their own age and so naturally gravitated towards each other. Both Reyna and Didu were taller than average, and had lighter hair colour than most Lemurians. Reyna had inherited her Atlantean blue eyes from her father and Didu, rather unusually for a Lemurian, had green eyes. Her unusual colouring and height had caused her to be somewhat of an outcast amongst her peers. Didu had overheard the other children whispering that perhaps her mother had taken an Atlantean lover, which had resulted in Didu's birth, but this was never confirmed. Nanni had told Didu not to concern herself with malicious gossip. However, the hurtful rumours did lead to Didu preferring Reyna's company to that of her other classmates.

Reyna excelled at school and was both courageous and physically strong. But she was quite a handful and was always getting herself and Didu into mischief. The two girls challenged many unspoken rules within their clan and Nanni often had to remind them both of the Lemurian rules of etiquette.

Didu and Reyna often visited Reyna's mother and father at the hybrid compound during holidays and both girls rapidly learned to speak the Atlantean language fluently. Although Didu did not know it at the time, this acquired skill was to prove invaluable in her future life.

Although Reyna and Didu were often in trouble for their high-spirited pranks, Reyna's problems really began when the girls commenced their initial training in the psychic and empathic skills, so essential to the Lemurian way of life, at age ten. Despite her sharp intellect and superior reasoning skills,

Reyna just couldn't find the still place within her own mind, which was the essential first step in the development of these skills. Her mind was like a chattering monkey and she had absolutely no patience with sitting still and going within. She preferred to be outside, playing and running and getting up to mischief.

Didu, on the other hand, found that she really excelled at these lessons and she discovered within herself a real hunger for knowledge and for a deepening spiritual connection. As a result, the girls gradually began to drift apart. Didu started to lose interest in Reyna's games and began to spend more and more time honing her telepathic and psychic skills, whilst Reyna found herself chafing at the restrictions placed upon her physical expressions by her schooling. Despite this, she very much wanted to be selected to be trained in the mystery school and was devastated when she wasn't selected, whereas Didu was.

Suddenly Didu's childhood friend began shunning her and, when they were together, Reyna would often make nasty, biting comments, which destroyed much of Didu's pleasure in her achievement of being selected.

Reyna was jealous, pure and simple, and she had no way of knowing what to do with these unfamiliar emotions. Her Lemurian upbringing had not provided her with the necessary skills to deal with negative emotions, which were completely alien to the empathic Lemurian people. When Didu's sister Lemma was selected as the adept for that year, it was the final straw. Reyna decided that she would go and live with her mother and father in the compound and make new friends. She simply couldn't bear being around Didu and Lemma any longer, as they both reminded her of what she could never be. She also had no interest in furthering her studies with the Lemurians, as these skills did not come naturally to her.

However, after a few months, Reyna found that living in the compound was almost just as bad. She felt completely alone and out of place and she quickly realised that her mother and father weren't really interested in raising a child. Her mother, because it was not in her culture to both give birth to, and raise, a child, and her father because he was too involved in the political intrigues and power struggles required to develop a successful career in Atlantean society.

Reyna felt as if she belonged nowhere and so she decided that she would try and make her own way in the world. Her father had told her about the Atlantean monastery schools and Reyna decided that, if she couldn't be a Lemurian adept, then she would try to become an Atlantean novice instead. The problem was that Atlantean schools also had a very strict selection process for their novices, who would then be trained to potentially be selected as priests and priestesses at the end of the training. These religious leaders were the ruling class of Atlantean society and held great power and wealth; all of which Reyna wanted for herself. After all, she believed that she deserved it, by dint of her much-celebrated superior intellect and abilities.

Reyna decided that the best place to learn about the ins-and-outs, and to position herself to be potentially selected as a novice, was in the schools themselves. Her father had had a childhood friend who was, at that time, a head teacher at one of the schools and, through this contact, Reyna was able to gain employ at one of the schools as a servant. She used her father's name only and did not share the information that she had a Lemurian mother, which would have instantly disqualified her from the job. She would bide her time, observe and learn. She was nothing if not smart and ambitious. If anyone could do it, she could!

And so Reyna began her job as an assistant in the kitchen of the largest monastery school two months before Lemma's initiation ceremony. She quickly made friends with her fellow servants and was much appreciated by the rest of the kitchen staff for her quick wit, her boundless energy and enthusiasm and for her physical strength. Despite this, she was still just a servant, who was mostly ignored by the novices and the teachers.

One morning, as Reyna was serving breakfast to the novices, she overheard two girls discussing the myths they had heard about the mysterious Lemurian initiation ceremony. Reyna saw an opportunity to draw attention to herself. After all, she knew all about the Lemurian initiation ceremonies, having attended five in total, since her sixth birthday. However, she had to be careful, as she didn't want the students to know that she was half Lemurian. If that became common knowledge, then any chances she might have at being accepted as a student in future would disappear.

"*I've heard that the moonlit ceremonies are held on the secluded beach just beyond the Sentinels, which are the giant sandstone cliffs that guard the entrance to the Bay of Porpoises. The ceremonies must be held in a sacred place in which the four elements are represented and this beach fulfils that criteria,*" Reyna said.

"*Really? How do you know that?*" asked one of the girls with interest, as both girls turned to stare at Reyna.

"*I... I... uh, overheard two Lemurian slaves discussing it in the marketplace,*" said Reyna, terrified now of the consequences of her impulsive words. Of course she knew that no Lemurians would ever discuss the sacred location of the initiation ceremonies. This was a very closely guarded secret. Lemurians knew that they were at risk whenever they emerged from their tunnels and so the annual initiation ceremony was a matter of extreme secrecy and, in fact, the location was changed every year. However, just before she had left her Lemurian clan two months earlier, Reyna had indeed overheard two of the Elders discussing the location of that year's rites. She had known about it before most of the clan had even been informed which, for security reasons, only happened the day before the actual event.

Suddenly Reyna was overwhelmed with remorse that she had shared this secret. She hoped that the two students would forget all about what she had told them. But alas, this was not to be, as one of the girls mentioned it to her father, who was involved in the Atlantean slave trade. Reyna's childish desire to be noticed was to have far-reaching repercussions...

Didu was awakened out of her reverie by the awareness that the initiation ceremony had begun. As usual, the rituals commenced with the procession of the Council into the place of meeting. As the thirteen white-robed Council members entered the circle, the people stood and remained standing until the Council members had been seated on a raised dais at the Northern side of the clearing, facing the ocean. Once the people were seated, Councilwoman Henda, the spokeswoman of the Council and a beloved neighbour of Didu's family, opened the proceedings by welcoming the people and by reminding those present of the history and purpose of the ritual that would follow...

Almost a hundred years before this time, a young Lemurian girl named Soni was exploring the caves at the foot of the mountain when she slipped from a rock face and fell, tumbling down a tunnel, deep into the heart of the mountain. She was to remain missing for a month, during which time her clan would believe that she had either been captured as a slave or killed by wild animals. When Soni emerged from the cave, she was to bring a message to her people that would change the course of their history and would set in motion the next step of their evolution.

When Soni regained consciousness, she found herself in a cavern lit by strange, flickering green lights. A voice spoke to her, deep within her heart, "*Soni, you have been chosen to bring a message to your people. The time of your people is rapidly coming to an end. The time of your slavery and suffering at the hands of your aggressors will soon be over. The time for the ascension of your people to a new dimension will soon be upon you.*"

Soni was terrified and she said, "*But, why me? I'm just an ordinary girl. I'm not anyone important and I might get the message wrong or forget it!*"

The voice replied, "*Soni, I am not currently in bodily form, but I am Eva, the guiding spirit of your people. You have been selected to bring this message to your people because you are courageous and because you are tenacious. You won't give up until you have been heard and until what I am asking of you and of your people has been achieved.*"

"*But... I don't understand! What are you asking of us?*" whispered Soni.

"*Soni, before you leave this cave, you will be given the secrets of immortality. You will be taught how to physically, mentally and spiritually prepare a select group of young people to receive these secrets at the end of their training. You will return to your people, and, using the Council to assist you, select six young people to train. Over a period of six years, you will train these young people and, at the end of that time, one will be selected to undergo the final initiation to become an adept. You and this first adept will then leave the tribe for good and take up residence in this place where the Great Work will commence. Some of the remaining five students will then train the next group of young people and this will continue for one hundred years, with one adept joining the group every year until a critical mass has been achieved. This will eventually result in the ascension of all the remaining members of your tribe to a new level of consciousness.*"

As Soni listened in amazement to the voice of Eva in her heart, she suddenly became aware of a bright white light beginning to illuminate the dark cavern and she gasped in astonishment to see that the cavern was actually an enormous, underground cathedral, with intricate carvings on the walls and elaborate buttresses supporting a massive, sky-blue, domed roof, high above.

"*Soni, this will be your home when you return in six years time, accompanied by the very first adept,*" said the voice of Eva in her heart. "*This is the place where you will begin the Great Work together.*"

"*But, how will I find this place again?*" asked Soni.

"*You will be guided, my child, in this, as in all things. Your life has a very important purpose. You are to be the bringer of the message of salvation for your people. You are also to become the first immortal."*

And then the light became blindingly bright and Soni gasped as her entire being was suffused with light. Every cell and fibre of her body became imbued with light and she was transformed. A massive body of knowledge and higher consciousness was imparted to her and when she finally emerged from the cave, she was no longer the same girl who had entered the cave a month earlier.

"And that, my dear people, is the story of how our mystery school began and also of how the adepts have been working for almost a century at elevating the consciousness of our people. My friends, tonight I take great pleasure in introducing you to Lemma, our latest adept, and one of the last few. Lemma, who will, in the grand tradition, be initiated tonight and who will join Soni and the other immortals in their Great Work in the stone monastery in the heart of the mountain. Soon, my dear people, we will have reached a critical mass of adepts, who will assist us in ascending our consciousness so that we may leave this place for good."

With that, Henda gestured to the young woman who had appeared in the centre of the circle and then took her seat on the dais to thunderous applause. Lemma waited in the centre of the circle until the applause had died down, her young face focussed in intense concentration. This would be the dance of her lifetime. She waited until there was not a sound to be heard in the gathered throng. The crowd held its collective breath for an infinite moment of silence...

And then Lemma began to dance. She danced to remind her people of their history and of their connection to each other and to Mother Earth. She danced to tell of their brilliant future when they would all ascend out of this place and be released from the shackles of their mortal bodies. Lemma danced... the past, the present and the future.

Didu was brought back to the present as the dancing and the chanting abruptly ended, as if in response to some silent commend. Lemma, her chest heaving from the exertion of the dance, quivering with exhaustion and dripping with perspiration, waited for a long moment, before slowly turning to face the Council of Elders. Despite her obvious physical exhaustion, she exuded an aura of power and control. Her training and natural aptitude was evident in her bearing and in her shining eyes. It was clear to all gathered that she was attuned, a worthy bearer of the ancient wisdom of the people.

And then, finally, the Spokeswoman stood once more. *"Lemma, you have admirably acquitted yourself of your task. You have danced your deep knowledge of the history, the present and the future of our people. Over the past six years you have proven yourself to be worthy of contributing to the Great Work. Now, the time has come to dedicate yourself to this goal.*

Lemma, are you ready to leave the clan of your birth and join your immortal family in working toward the ascension of our entire race? Are you prepared to sacrifice the personal in favour of the collective good?"

The silence in the place of gathering was absolute as the tribe awaited Lemma's response. She still had an opportunity to decide to remain with her family, which would mean that there would be no adept leaving for the mountain that year. This had happened only once in the past, but there was no shame attached to this decision, as all knew that the price of this sacrifice was very high.

And then Lemma spoke, her clear, young voice ringing out in the still night air, "*I will!*" and a collective sigh arose and echoed throughout the clearing. Now, all that remained would be for Lemma to seal her vow by drinking the sacrament from the sacred vessel. After this, she would bid her clan farewell and would immediately depart for the monastery. They would never see her physical body again in this lifetime, but they would know that she would be working with her new family to secure the future of the entire tribe and this would bring them comfort.

Henda herself poured the sacrament into the bowl and descended from the dais, careful not to spill a single drop of the brew. The sacrament was prepared according to a secret recipe that had been taught to Soni by Eva in the cave. It was said that only those trained for six years in the mystery school could drink the brew and survive. For the one chosen to become an adept, the brew would facilitate their process of becoming immortal, which would finally be completed once they entered the stone monastery under the mountain.

Lemma knelt and Henda handed her the bowl, with a deep bow. It was a mark of great respect and appreciation for the sacrifice made by Lemma and for the work that she would do in future.

As per tradition, Lemma lifted the bowl high above her head and uttered silent prayers of dedication and thanks to the Goddess, before slowly lifting the bowl to her lips and drinking deeply, right down to the very last drop.

The only sound Didu could hear was the breaking of the waves and her own heartbeat booming in her ears. Lemma remained still, her head bowed for a few minutes, before taking the pitcher of water from Henda and thoroughly rinsing the bowl. Then she arose and walked over to her sister, Didu, and handed her the bowl. Didu accepted the bowl with tears streaming down her cheeks. She knew that this precious relic would be the only tangible memento that she would have of her sister to comfort her in the years to come. Lemma hugged Didu and their Grandmother one last time. And then she turned to leave the place of gathering to commence her long trip up the mountain to her new home.

Returning to the village after the ceremony, tightly clutching the ceremonial bowl to her chest, Didu felt both exhausted and very sad. But she kept trying to be brave, as she knew that her sister was fulfilling her highest destiny. She also knew that if all went according to her plan, she would, in six years, be reunited with her sister in the mountain monastery. Didu knew that she would have to hold tight to that thought in order to help her get through the next few years of loneliness. She made a vow to herself to work as hard as she possibly could to ensure that she would be the student chosen as the adept at the end of her training.

It was already very late, as Didu's friends and neighbours walking in the group with her had been the very last to leave the place of gathering. They had stayed behind to clear all traces of the ceremony and, when they had left, there had been no sign of the events that had taken place there that evening. This was to ensure the secrecy and future safety of their gatherings. The group was subdued and quiet. This was in stark contrast to the air of excited anticipation that had prevailed on their journey to the place of gathering. The ceremony always reminded the people that they were the ones left behind to age and to die, whereas those who were selected to be trained in the mystery school and were able to make it through the arduous selection process as an adept would live forever in the mountain monastery.

Suddenly Didu became aware of a subtle change in the air; a frisson of alertness, tinged with a metallic edge of fear. She could sense that the adults were wary and anticipating some danger. At the very edges of her awareness Didu too could sense some new presence; a darkness; a threatening shadow.

"What is it, Nanni?" Didu asked her Grandmother in a whisper, but for once Nanni didn't patiently answer her question but turned to whisper rapidly and urgently to Councilwoman Hedda, who was walking beside her.

Before Didu could discover what was happening, the group of adults moved to form a protective shield around the children and their pace picked up considerably. Didu began to feel really frightened. The group was now moving so fast that some of the smaller children were struggling to keep up. Didu tried reaching out with her mind to access the thoughts of the adults, but, unusually, their thoughts were shielded from her and it was this, more than anything else, that caused her heart to pound against her ribs in alarm. All Didu could sense was the overwhelming stench of fear and apprehension.

Then, just as the group finally reached the copse of trees adjacent to the hidden tunnel leading to their home, several blood-curdling screams rent the still night air and suddenly the group was surrounded by six huge, fierce-looking men, wielding weapons. It was an Atlantean raid! This then was the bitter harvest from Reyna's betrayal of the secret location of the initiation ceremony.

The Lemurian adults formed a tight circle around the children, but it was hopeless from the start, despite their greater numbers, as they were unarmed, far smaller and lighter in stature than their aggressors and not adept at fighting or in protecting themselves. Didu watched in horror as her Grandmother, Hedda and the other adults were easily beaten aside. Then a mountain of a man with long, white, matted hair picked her up in one arm, laughing at her with an open mouth full of broken, brown-stained teeth. With Didu under one arm and another, smaller child under the other, her captor ran off into the trees, followed by his five companions, each bearing their own live trophies.

The Green Lady paused at this point in the narrative and I glanced up, to catch a shadow of sadness crossing her face. I realised that she was deeply invested in this story and that these memories cost her considerable pain to recount.

"*How terrifying that must have been!*" I softly said.

"*Yes, and far worse was yet to come,*" she replied. "*But, these experiences were necessary in order to become who I am today. Shall we continue with the story?*"

Didu was sitting on a cold, hard, black step, made of some kind of stone that she had never before encountered, looking up the flight of stairs leading into an imposing building, decorated with massive stone pillars. For a girl raised in a place of soft warmth, constant gentle touch and dimly-lit underground caverns, this place was especially hard and cold and the harsh sun hurt her eyes. She was still clutching the initiation bowl to her chest, holding on for dear life to the only reminder she had left of her home and of her family. Her captor had deposited her on these steps a short while earlier, with strict instructions, in execrable, barely comprehensible Lemurian, not to move if she valued her life. Except for the small boy, Hef, who had been her fellow abductee, Didu had not seen the other children of her clan since the raid. Hef had been handed over to a large, red-faced woman outside the back door of an impressive home half an hour before Didu had been left on the stairs. But their captor had followed such a complicated route to get to where she now was that Didu knew for certain that she would never again be able to find the house at which Hef had been left.

Didu had no inclination to move from her current location, but rather crouched, huddled up in a tiny ball on the step. She had been told that her new owner would be arriving shortly to collect her and she was unsure of whether to feel dread or relief at this fact.

But after more than an hour on the step, Didu's youth and natural optimism began to reassert itself and she started to take notice of her surroundings. After all, she reasoned, she would need to pay attention to what was going on around her if she wanted to have any chance at all of escape.

There were many people coming-and-going, up and down the stairs: servants and merchants and other, clearly wealthy, individuals, all dressed in fine and colourful clothing and all appearing very self-assured and imposing. The women had long, elaborately dressed, blonde hair, often threaded through with sparkling jewels and everyone was very tall and powerfully built. Didu felt tiny and insignificant and her heart leapt as a very large black bird perched on a higher step suddenly squawked loudly, causing her to jump up in alarm.

The initiation bowl slipped from her hands and smashed into shards on the ground below. Didu burst into tears as her heart drowned in the hopelessness of her situation. Her last connection to her clan and her sister... gone! She knew, in her heart of hearts, that the chances of her ever escaping this place were diminishingly small. Everything which had been important to her in her short life thus far now seemed childish, laughable and not good enough for this place. She felt completely lost and diminished and she howled her fear and loss and loneliness.

Then, after a while, her tears dried up. There seemed to be no point to crying when it wouldn't alter a single thing about her situation.

A short while later a woman appeared at the top of the flight of stairs. Didu stared at her in amazement. Her clothing was ornate and decorated with sparkling stones and shimmering gold and silver thread. Hers was, by far, the most elaborate clothing that Didu had yet seen that morning. The woman was tall and haughty and her nose wrinkled in disgust as she took in Didu's plain white robe, dirty bare feet, tear-stained cheeks and tangled hair.

"*Is this it?*" she asked in imperious tones, her voice high-pitched and cold. "*Surely Wen could have found us a better specimen than this?*" Clearly the woman was not aware that Didu could understand the Atlantean language. Didu's cheeks reddened with embarrassment at the dismissive tone in the woman's voice.

She scrambled to her feet, noticing as she did so that the lady was accompanied by two other women, dressed in far less ornate clothing. "*Well, I suppose she'll have to do until Wen can catch something better. Kayla, take her to the washrooms and scrub that grime off her and get her some* clean clothing. And please, for goodness sake, shave that ratty, flea-infested hair off her head! Then take her to the kitchens. She can start off by learning to help cook. Perhaps a few years of training could turn her into something useful."

As the larger of the two servants grabbed Didu's arm and pulled her up the staircase and through a side door leading into the building, Didu felt overwhelmed by fear and loneliness. She knew that all her plans to become an adept would probably never come to fruition now. Was it her destiny to be a common slave?

Didu awoke before dawn, just as she had every morning for the past two years. Despite the cold, she immediately stood up, folding and stowing her blanket and sleeping mat and rapidly dressing herself for the day's work. Around her the other serving girls were similarly occupied in readying themselves for yet another day of the labour required to keep the massive household going, but Didu didn't speak to any of them. She had learnt that, as a Lemurian slave, she was lower than the lowest of them and that any friendship overtures from her would be harshly rebuffed. It was easiest and safest to keep her head down and just get on with her work.

She also knew from bitter experience that dawdling would earn her a cuff around the ears at best and a day without food at worst. So Didu hurried through her ablutions, before presenting herself to the head servant to have her head shaved, as was required of her, every single morning. Didu herself was not trusted to do the job properly or to have access to the razor. The purpose of her shaved head was twofold: firstly to indicate her slave status and secondly to minimise her chances of "contaminating" the food with which she came into contact. That morning the head servant was impatient and nicked Didu's scalp in two places, but she didn't complain, merely biting her lip against the pain and then bustling down the stairs of the servants' quarters to reach the kitchen the moment the last bristle of hair was removed.

The cook was in a foul mood, as per usual for the breakfast stint, and a dropped spoon earned Didu a stinging smack to the side of her head. Didu's natural gifts of intuition meant that she could sense when the cook was going to strike her, and so she flinched twice, once in anticipation and once when the actual blow arrived. Over the past two years, she had learnt which kinds of behaviour caused the cook's temper to flare up and Didu did her best to keep her superior in an even temper. Consequently, the number of beatings she had to endure had considerably lessened.

Three gruelling hours later and the family had been served their breakfast and the kitchen cleaned in readiness for the preparation of the afternoon meal. Finally Didu and the other servants were served a meagre breakfast of thin broth made from boiled bones, and bread crusts, washed down with ale. Although this was the servant meal that had been approved by the mistress of the house, all the servants knew that there would always be an abundance of leftovers from the family's meals by the end of the day. No high-born Atlantean would ever contemplate eating leftovers. Officially these leftovers were fed to the pigs, but in reality the servants polished them off.

As a slave, Didu was allowed to eat whatever was left after the servants had eaten their fill. Before her enslavement, Didu had never eaten any animal products, but now she ate absolutely everything she was given. Her daily, physically demanding work meant that she was almost constantly hungry.

As Didu was getting up from the breakfast table to begin the work of preparing the vegetables for the afternoon meal, she was intercepted by the cook. *"Girl, I need some bitter herbs for the luncheon soup. Grisa forgot to get them from the market this morning and Madame specifically requested my special orze soup for her luncheon guests today. Hurry now, get to the market quick! I can't spare any of the other girls as they need to polish the best silverware for the meal."*

Didu had often felt hurt by the Madame's insistence that she not be allowed to touch any of the silverware or crockery from which the family ate, as she would, apparently, contaminate it with her "dirty paws". But, for once, this discrimination was working in her favour. She relished the thought of a rare, brief outing to the market and she ran to fetch her shawl against the cold weather.

Once outside, Didu breathed deeply of the cool, misty morning air. Her spirits lifted at the unexpected pleasure of being out of the kitchen for an hour and she began to walk briskly in the direction of the market. Passing her on all sides were bustling citizens clad in rich, ornate clothing. The Atlanteans certainly knew how to live pampered and luxurious lives, but Didu thought that she would exchange the opulence of their lives in a heartbeat for the quiet, simple, but deeply connected life she had enjoyed with her clan.

For a moment Didu was overwhelmed by the familiar feelings of sadness and loss. She had not heard a word from her family and she had no way of knowing whether her Grandmother and the other adults had survived the ambush two years earlier. She had never discovered where any of the other children taken as slaves on the same night she had been abducted had ended up. She only knew that no Lemurian child taken as a slave had ever returned home.

Didu was just pleased that Lemma had left for the monastery before the attack had occurred. At least she knew that her sister would be safe and working for the good of the tribe as a whole. But Didu knew that there was very little chance of her seeing any of her clan or friends ever again. As an adept this would have been her fate too, but that would have been six years in the future. And at least then she would have gone willingly and would have spent the intervening years being trained in a variety of techniques and arcane knowledge, which would now forever be closed to her.

Briefly Didu considered an escape attempt. However, from two previous such attempts she knew that her chances at success were zero and that she would be severely punished for her attempt. She still bore on her back the scars from the brutal whippings she had endured on the two previous occasions. The city gates were heavily guarded and all vehicles, animals and pedestrians leaving the city were thoroughly searched. Also, if she tried to hide somewhere, she would eventually be picked up by one of the city watchmen and she did not possess the necessary papers that would prove her citizenship. A third attempt would earn her more than a whipping. She would probably be imprisoned. And the other servants had relished telling Didu horrifying stories of the atrocities that occurred in the prisons, particularly to young women. No, she really was alone and virtually friendless in this harsh place, but at least she did have a place to sleep and food to eat.

Didu knew, from bitter experience, that this line of thought led nowhere good. So she shook off her sadness and focussed on getting to the market as quickly as she could so that there might be a few moments spare to spend as she wanted to before she would be expected back at the mansion.

A large chattering group of young Atlanteans dressed in red novice robes passed Didu. Atlantis was ruled by an elite group of priests and priestesses. Similar to the Lemurians, specially selected young people were trained for years in arcane knowledge and techniques at one of four monastery schools in the city. At the age of eighteen, the top students of each year underwent an initiation ritual which inducted them into the ruling elite. The ritual was shrouded in mystery, but it was widely known that the ruling priests and priestesses had supernatural abilities not possessed by ordinary people. They had access to deep knowledge, they could read minds and they could influence peoples' opinions and beliefs with their thoughts. This made them able to rule the general populace with absolute domination and control. Didu wondered what happened during their rituals. Where did they obtain their power and knowledge? Didu wished that she might have access to even a fraction of that knowledge, as she would immediately use it to get back home to her people.

One of the novices, a girl no older than Didu, turned to her friend and Didu caught a brief glimpse of her shaven head beneath her hood. All novices, priests and priestesses were required to shave their heads to symbolise their renunciation of the temptations of the world. Didu reflected bitterly on the irony of her own shaven head, which, in her case, denoted her lowly status as a slave, whereas the same lack of hair indicated the elevated status of the ruling class of priests and priestesses.

Reaching the marketplace, Didu quickly located the herbalist's stall and requested the necessary herbs. The herbalist added the cost of the herbs to the account of the mansion because Didu, as a Lemurian slave, was not trusted to either carry or handle money. As he handed Didu the herbs with a sneer, he made sure not to touch her fingers, for fear of contaminating himself. Didu hardly even noticed the herbalist's disdain, being very accustomed to such treatment by now.

With the packet of herbs safely tucked into the pocket in her robe, Didu made her way to the beautiful gardens in the centre of the city. This was the one place where she felt safe and, momentarily, happy. Walking along an orderly avenue of evergreen conifers, Didu basked in the beauty of the park. Although it was still quite cold, the snow had melted and the first small spring flowers and tentative pale-green shoots had begun to make their appearance. Approaching the conservatory, Didu looked around for a sign of Pey. Yes, there he was!

Pey was an old Lemurian who had also been taken captive when he was a boy. He had worked as a gardener in the city ever since. Over the two years of her own captivity, Didu had met up with Pey on a handful of occasions, whenever she had been able to steal a few moments of respite in the gardens. She had first become aware of Pey when the Madame and the children had decided to have a picnic in the gardens a few months after Didu had been taken captive. Didu and several other servants had been ordered to carry and serve the picnic. Standing to attention at the edge of the picnic blanket, waiting to be called upon to refill a glass or plate, Didu had become aware of being observed. Turning her head, she had encountered the empathic gaze of the gardener's chocolate-brown eyes and had immediately known that he was of her own people.

Later, as her mistress and the children dozed in the sun, Didu had managed to have a whispered conversation with Pey. She had discovered that Pey had been working in the gardens for over fifty years. He was trusted to manage his own time now and was left alone for the most part. He found joy and fulfilment in creating the beautiful formal gardens. Although Pey was the only friend that Didu had in the city, she found spending time with him to be a bittersweet experience, as he reminded her of the fact that escape was impossible and that she too would probably spend her entire life in servitude, all alone in this strange city. Pey had, however, always reminded her not to give up hope, but to try and find joy in the little things in her life.

"*Greetings, Pey,*" Didu called out and Pey looked up, his face lighting up with joy to see his young friend.

"*Greetings, little one! My, but you do get prettier by the day.*"

"*Much good that'll do me,*" scoffed Didu. "*My chances at having a normal life are zero. And I certainly wouldn't want to wed one of the beastly Atlanteans! Anyway, no self-respecting Atlantean man would want a puny, weak and inferior Lemurian specimen such as myself.*"

"*You're wrong, you know, Didu,*" said Pey in an unusually serious tone. "*You have grown tall and strong in your years here. Perhaps it's the non-vegetarian diet; perhaps the exposure to sunshine. With your green eyes and dressed in the clothing of an Atlantean, no-one would be able to tell the difference. You are a beautiful young woman, Didu. Any man, Atlantean or Lemurian, would be pleased to have you.*"

Didu was about to object to this opinion when a strange whistling sound caught her attention. Both Didu and Pey looked up and were astonished to discover giant fireballs raining down from the heavens. In the distance they could now see that massive flaming rocks were crashing into buildings and market stalls and the air was suddenly rent with screams of agony and shrieks of fear.

"*Didu! Quick, this way,*" called Pey, pulling Didu away from the conservatory and behind a large clump of bushes. And just in time too, as a massive boulder crashed into the conservatory, right next to where they had been standing a moment earlier. A flying shard of glass sliced into Didu's forehead as she turned to follow her companion. "*Hurry, in here!*" said Pey, pulling Didu by the hand into a tunnel, whose opening had been obscured by the bushes. Crouching low, Didu and Pey crawled into the tunnel and hunkered down in a shallow bunker, a few metres from the entrance.

"*Pey, what is going on?*" asked Didu, in a small, frightened voice, using the hem of her robe to staunch the blood running down her face from the cut in her forehead.

"*I'm not entirely sure, little one, but I do remember hearing legends of massive balls of fire descending from the heavens when I was a small boy. There was a very old woman in my clan who used to tell us tales of how, when she had been a little girl, she had witnessed such events with her own eyes. She told us that the fireballs always heralded in change; a new beginning for our people. But, until today, I guess had always dismissed those stories as merely myths.*"

"*Well, thank the Goddess that we have a safe place to hide until it's over,*" said Didu breathlessly. "*What is this place, by the way?*"

"*It's just a small refuge I built over the years for when I would most need it. Seems like that day has come!*" said Pey, the whites of his eyes gleaming in the darkness of the tunnel.

"*A good Lemurian makes sure that there is always a tunnel to escape into when needed.*"

Didu and Pey stayed in the tunnel for the rest of the afternoon, listening to the muted sounds of chaos and destruction in the distance. When night fell and the air began to cool, Pey rummaged behind a pile of rocks at the back of the tunnel and handed Didu a few dry biscuits and a canister of stale, dusty water, as well as a cloak made of red fabric.

"*What...? This is a novice's cloak, Pey! Where did you get it?*" Didu asked, her voice rising in excitement.

"*People leave many interesting things in the park, you know. And even novices get up to all kinds of illicit behaviour when they think they are alone and unobserved,*" chuckled Pey. Didu smiled to herself and gratefully curled up snug and warm inside the capacious robe.

She must have fallen asleep because the next thing she knew, Pey was gently shaking her, whispering, "*Didu, it's time to get moving now, my child. Today might just be the day!*"

"*What...? Where am I? What's happening?*" asked Didu, blearily wiping the sleep from her eyes and yawning and stretching the kinks out of her spine from sleeping on the cold, hard earth floor.

"*You need to get going, Didu. The rain of fire has stopped, but things will be in disarray and there may just be an opportunity for you to escape!*" Pey's words penetrated Didu's consciousness like a bucket of ice-cold water on a winter's morning. She immediately arose and rapidly followed him out of the tunnel and into the pale, watery, early-morning sunlight.

A scene of utter devastation met her eyes. The entire inner-city garden had been destroyed. Half-broken trees and crushed bushes adorned with broken glass and splintered trellises littered the ground. All the flowers had been obliterated and the wooden garden shack had been reduced to a smouldering pile of timbers. Pey didn't even stop for a moment to mourn the destruction of his life's work.

"Come, come quickly! Didu, wrap that robe tightly around yourself. Your destiny awaits, child!" Pey rapidly led Didu in the direction of the city gates, past burning buildings and crushed statues. Past ruined temples and smouldering market barrows, with produce scattered all over the street and people milling everywhere, crying and moaning in a state of shock. As Didu and Pey passed the mansion where she had spent the last two years of her life, Didu gasped with shock. The entire building had been reduced to a pile of rubble. It had been a direct hit and there was no-one to be seen. In her soul Didu knew that the entire household had been killed. If she had not been sent to the market for herbs, she too would now be dead.

"Come child, you can't stay here. It's not safe!" said Pey, just as a massive explosion erupted further down the street and then Didu and Pey were swept along by wave after wave of panicked people running to escape the blast.

Wherever Pey and Didu went, people were running around like ants, but when they finally reached the city gates, they discovered that security was tighter than ever. The guards had placed the entire city in lock-down and no-one was allowed to either leave or enter the city without a signed, sealed writ of permission from the council itself.

"Control must be maintained at all costs!" they heard the captain of the guard yelling at his troops. *"No looting will be tolerated. The city must be contained, and until order is*

restored, these gates must not be breached. No exceptions whatsoever!"

Muttering under his breath, Pey led Didu down a back alley away from the city gates. Stopping suddenly in a stone archway, Pey turned Didu to face him and whispered urgently, "*Didu, do you trust me?*"

"*Of course I trust you - we're kin after all. Why? What's going on, Pey?*" asked Didu, staring at her friend with wide, frightened eyes.

"*I have a new plan, Didu. I'm going to secure a future for you, even if it's not the future you would have chosen for yourself. It will be a good deal better than a future of servile drudgery. This is your one-and-only chance and you need to take it! Come with me now.*" Pey grabbed Didu's hand and pulled her through a labyrinth of passageways in which the buildings were mostly still intact, until finally they reached a large stone building.

"*It's the main monastery school,*" breathed Didu who had had the building pointed out to her by another servant on a previous occasion. "*What are we doing here?*"

"*Didu, this is your one chance at a decent future,*" said Pey with some urgency, turning the girl to look at him. "*You have the novice's robe. Your hair is shaved off. I know you don't have the papers of a citizen, but all systems will be in disarray for some time and you can simply claim that your papers were destroyed when your monastery home burned down. If you act traumatised enough, people will believe you. No-one will anyway believe that a Lemurian slave girl would have the courage or the ability to try something like this. Fortunately you speak fluent Atlantean. Pretend that you have lost your memory due to head trauma. That cut on your forehead looks bad enough. If you play it up, they will take pity*"

on you. *You have the looks and bearing of a noble Atlantean.*
Just keep your hair shorn to the scalp at all times. They'll think
you are just being extra pious and there's no reason why they
wouldn't believe you. Come now, this is your only chance!" So
saying, Pey pounded at the door of the school, which was soon
opened by a harried-looking middle-aged woman.

"*Oh, my poor child, are you alright? You're injured -*
come inside right away," she exclaimed, pulling Didu through
the doorway. Didu turned around to find Pey, but he had
vanished and so she allowed herself to be led through to a
warm and comfortable room in which several other young
people, all dressed in red robes and all covered in mud and
scratches were being attended to by a number of helpers.

Soon Didu found herself seated with a cup of hot,
spiced milk in her hands, her face being gently wiped with a
warm, wet cloth whilst the cut on her forehead was cleaned
and dressed by a pair of gentle hands. It had been a very long
time since Didu had been treated with kindness and this,
combined with the trauma of the past day, caused the child to
break down sobbing, which made her story of memory loss
seem very plausible.

Didu allowed herself to be comforted by one of the
helpers and then she finished her cup of milk. As a hand
reached out to take her empty cup, Didu looked up and gasped
to find herself staring into the eyes of her childhood best
friend, Reyna. Recognition lit up Reyna's face, followed by
some powerful emotion, which Didu couldn't recognise; but it
was actually intense guilt and shame that twisted Reyna's
features into a mask of pain.

Reyna had discovered the consequences of her
betrayal when she had returned to the hybrid compound for a
short break to visit her parents. She had been devastated to

discover that Nanni, who had raised her with such kindness and patience, had been killed in the ambush and that Councilwoman Henda and one of the other adults had been so severely injured that they had both had to retire from their jobs. The rest of the adults had all sustained injuries of varying severity. No-one in the compound knew where the eight children, including Didu, had landed up.

Reyna had been overcome by guilt and shame at her role in the disaster. She knew that she would never be able to forgive herself for what she had done. She was never to visit her Lemurian clan members again, as she simply didn't have the courage to face them, given her knowledge of her crime. She lost all ambition to be trained as a priestess and returned to her job in the monastery school an utterly changed girl. She no longer laughed and chatted with her fellow servants. She became silent and withdrawn and carried out her tasks with the minimum of fuss. Although she often thought of Didu, it was always with silent self-rebuke and she lacked the courage to try and find Didu in the city. What could she possibly say to her childhood friend? How could she ever make it up to her? After all, she had been personally responsible for the death of Didu's Grandmother and for Didu being taken as a slave.

However, as Reyna stared into Didu's desperate eyes, for the first time in the past two, hellish years, she began to see a glimmer of hope. The slightest possibility of a modicum of redemption.

Reyna turned to the nearest nun and said, "*Sister, I know this girl! She may have lost her memory, but I can tell you who she is!*"

Didu's heart leapt into her throat as she realised that her one chance at a different life was about to be destroyed.

However, she was astonished to hear the next words that emerged from Reyna's mouth.

"*Yes, sister! A month ago, when I delivered a message to the sisters at the South Gate Monastery, I encountered this girl in the gardens, where I was waiting for a response from the sisters. We had a brief discussion about the spring flowers. I seem to recall that her name is Deena.*" Reyna knew that the South Gate Monastery and all of its inhabitants had been destroyed by the meteorite shower of the previous day.

"*Oh, the poor child! I wonder how she managed to survive,*" gasped the nun. Didu looked into Reyna's eyes, her own eyes brimming with tears, and realised that she was safe - her friend would never betray her.

For the next four years, this monastery school was to be Didu's home.

Her teachers were, for the most part, kind and patient. Didu who, thanks to Reyna, was now known as Deena, having assumed the name and identity of one of the Atlantean novices who had died in the meteorite shower, now experienced the better parts of Atlantean culture. She realised that these people weren't all evil, as she had previously thought and been told by her Lemurian clan members. The Atlanteans actually had a well-developed culture and sophisticated religious practices. Deena was taught many new skills and useful knowledge that had been accumulated over millennia by the Atlanteans.

There came a time when Deena realised that she had not thought about her Lemurian friends and family for a very long time indeed. She had made several new friends and had acquired a new family in her classmates, in several of her teachers and some of the older students. Reyna, however, kept her distance and the girls rarely spoke because Reyna would keep her eyes averted and address Deena as "mistress" whenever they happened to run into each other. Deena gave up trying to find out why that was and simply got on with her new life. Although Deena did visit the remains of the city gardens several times, she never again encountered Pey and the gardens were eventually levelled and replaced by apartment buildings.

The years flew by and soon Deena was a young woman of eighteen, at the end of her schooling career and eligible for selection as a priestess into the ruling class of her adopted culture.

Deena's native intellect and her well-hidden natural telepathic and empathic talents had enabled her to qualify at the very top of her class. She had many friends and she had adapted well to her new life. In fact, she often forgot that she wasn't really an Atlantean, but rather a so-called inferior Lemurian. But sometimes at night, when she was alone in her bed, she would lie awake worrying that she would inadvertently reveal her origins. She feared losing her privileged status as a novice and being sent back to the kitchens as a slave.

But, in the deepest, most unexamined, most shadowed part of her heart, Deena feared even more being sent back to the community where she had spent the first twelve years of her life. She could no longer imagine living without the luxuries and the amenities to which she had grown accustomed. The thought of having to live like a primitive again in tunnels and caverns beneath the earth was enough to guarantee her silence and secrecy regarding her background. Every day that passed caused her to become further and further alienated from the culture into which she had been born. To her horror, she now often found herself laughing along with her classmates when they made jokes about the "backward" and "primitive" Lemurians. She was becoming a stranger, even to herself. Deena now felt as if she was two very different people, each being screened off from the other by a secret veil of shame inside of her own mind.

At the final graduation ceremony, the head teacher of the monastery school announced that Deena was one of the students who had been selected to further her studies as a novice priestess. This meant that she would effectively be groomed for a position of status and power in future; perhaps even the highest position of all - that of High Priestess of the Realm. Her training would now be accelerated and she would be inducted into certain occult mysteries that were only made known to those in the very highest echelons of power.

Deena was both exhilarated and appalled by this news. What had become of her? She hardly recognised herself! But when the Head Priest of the monastery held his hand out to her, she accepted it without hesitation and allowed herself to be led into the inner sanctum to complete her training.

Following the procession of priests and priestesses, Deena entered the vaulted stone temple. Five years had elapsed since her novice graduation ceremony and she had successfully completed the requisite training in all the occult knowledge available to the Atlantean High Order. She was about to undergo the final initiation ceremony; the process known as the Merging.

Deena was suffused with pride and terror in equal measures. There would be no turning back now. Tonight would seal her fate as one of the most powerful individuals in the entire Atlantean civilisation. After tonight she would be well on her way to occupying whichever position of unlimited power she chose. Already she had been approached by several competing clans to represent them at the highest levels of governance. She would have unlimited access to power and wealth and influence.

Underlying her pride in her achievements was abject terror, because she well knew that if the knowledge of her background were ever to become public knowledge, she would surely be executed. It would be considered an act of high treason for someone at her level to have originated from, what was considered to be, the inferior Lemurian slave-class. Deena comforted herself that there was no way anyone could possibly ever discover her origins. Pey the gardener was, for sure, long dead and she was absolutely convinced that Reyna would never betray her. Her Lemurian friends and clan couldn't possibly recognise the little kidnapped Lemurian girl in the stately, beautiful and all-powerful Priestess she would soon become.

Deena allowed herself a small inner congratulatory smile as she reflected on how she had successfully infiltrated the highest levels of power in Atlantean society. She had proven that she wasn't a nobody after all. She had access to unlimited wealth and power and she intended to fully use it! A life of luxury and ease and influence was her right... and indeed, her destiny.

The temple was filled with monks and nuns and novices, all chanting the words of the dedication. Deena and her fellow adepts gathered in a semi-circle on the raised dais around the candle-lit alter, where the present High Priest stood waiting, his hands resting on the Book of the Word.

After the usual prayers, hymns, sermon and dedications, the High Priest made the sign and the novices were led out of the temple by their teachers. The secret ritual could now finally commence.

Once the heavy temple doors had closed behind the teachers and students, the High Priest stepped closer to the adepts and intoned, "*Adepts of the One True Way, you have, by submitting to the training of the past five years and by successfully completing all the tasks and sacrifices assigned to you, reached the final moment of your old lives. From this moment onwards, you will die to your old life and will be reborn into a new life. A life that demands great sacrifice and service; but a life that also offers immense rewards and compensations. From this point onwards, there is no turning back and so I exhort you to examine your consciences. Be very sure that there is no reason whatsoever that you should not accept this burden of responsibility and privilege. Be very sure that this is, without a shadow of a doubt, what your heart and soul call you to do.*"

Deena's heart was pounding so hard that she was certain her fellow adepts would hear it. This was the moment... Now! From this point onwards there would be no turning back. If she achieved this milestone, none would ever gainsay her again. Terror of being unmasked alternated with pride and vanity at being chosen.

The High Priest waited. It seemed for an eternity. And then there was a commotion as one of Deena's fellow adepts stepped down, with a mumbled apology, from the raised dais and half stumbled, half ran, back down the aisle to exit via the heavy wooden doors. But Deena held firm and shortly thereafter the High Priest began the initiation ceremony for the remaining three adepts.

"As the adepts standing here before me are aware, much occult power and knowledge is made available to those selected to serve at the highest levels of power and influence. This is to enable them to direct and guide society in the direction of the greatest utility for the greatest number of citizens. Now, at this highest initiation, there is a final level of secret power that will be made available to these adepts. This is the power of the Merging. Once Merged, these adepts become the illuminated ones and will remain so for their natural lives. Only at the moment of death may the bond that we are about to create be broken. There is no turning back; no returning of the ultimate power that will lead to the compete transformation of the three adepts standing here before me today. Today, in this place, they will die to their old selves and be resurrected into their new, Godlike selves, with new Godlike powers of precognition, mind control, telekinesis, telepathy and many, many more. These powers shall be given to them through the act of willing surrender unto their own personal Peer. This is a discarnate being, which shall henceforth be joined together with each adept in an unbreakable soul-bond.

The adept shall provide their Peer with the experiences of incarnated, embodied life and allow the Peer to feed with them upon various energies associated with the physical form. In return, they shall receive the super-natural gifts which will give them great power. Great power, which shall be used wisely in the leadership positions to which they are entitled, by dint of their birth, their breeding, their training and their natural abilities and aptitude. This soul contract should never be taken lightly. The Merging holds certain physical dangers to those of weaker constitutions and it is not guaranteed that the adept will survive the arduous Merging process.

Now, in full knowledge of the gravity and dangers of the process that lies ahead, are you still willing to proceed? Deena, what say you?"

"*I am*," said Deena, her heart pounding in her ears as she heard her two fellow adepts, in turn, similarly affirm their willingness to proceed.

"*Then, each adept shall now, in turn, drink of the elixir in this goblet, which shall allow their souls to slumber for long enough to permit the successful merging.*"

The nuns and monks began to softly chant as a young nun stepped forward to take the hand of Enza, a tall, muscular young man with strong, chiselled features, and to lead him to the altar, where he was bidden to be seated. The High Priest handed the goblet to Enza, who drank deeply and then lay down upon the altar.

The High Priest took up the chant in a deep bass voice, followed by the other priests and priestesses. The chant grew louder and faster and Enza's body began to writhe and thrash around on the altar. Moans erupted from his lips and perspiration streamed down his face and torso. The chanting reached a fever pitch and Enza screamed in agony - one long, loud scream, before falling silent. The chanting stopped and the priests waited.

Deena was absolutely terrified. Enza appeared to be dead; he was lying silently on the altar and didn't seem to be breathing. But then, just when she felt as if her terror would drive her from the temple, Enza opened his eyes and very slowly sat up. Deena caught a glimpse of his eyes and a chill ran through the very marrow of her bones. This was no longer the Enza she had studied and sparred with for the past five years. He was someone, or something, completely different.

"*Yes, you're right. I am completely different,*" Deena heard the voice of Enza in her mind and her startled eyes flew to his face as she realised that he was now able to communicate telepathically with her. "*And that's the least of it!*" he spoke into her mind. "*You won't believe the power and knowledge and abilities I now have! This feels fantastic!*" Enza crowed, directly into Deena's mind as he stood up and stepped aside to allow the nun to lead the next adept to the altar.

The High Priest turned to the next adept, a slender and wiry young man called Biba. Deena could see that Biba was just as terrified as she was. His wide, darting eyes convinced her that he would prefer to be just about anywhere else at this moment, but that he would die before letting anyone else know that. Biba drank deeply from the goblet and, in turn, fell back onto the altar in a deep slumber. The chanting began again but Deena was convinced, somewhere deep within her being, that something wasn't quite right. Although the chanting of the priests reached the same levels as before, Biba didn't make a sound, nor did his body move. Eventually, upon a signal from the High Priest, the chanting stopped and two priests stepped forward to assist Biba, but Deena already knew that he was gone. Biba's body was carried out of the temple by the two priests and, after a moment or two of silence, the High Priest turned to Deena.

"*The Merging is an arduous process that requires the highest levels of courage, purity and strength. Only the most deserving will prevail. None would blame you if you decided to defer your Merging for another time,*" he said in a solemn tone. Looking around, Deena could see a faint smile hovering at the corners of Enza's lips. He would absolutely love it if she were to withdraw from the proceedings now, she thought. She would never give him that satisfaction. Never!

"*I will proceed,*" she stated in a calm, steady voice, that surprised even herself. The High Priest looked rather taken-aback, but beckoned to the young nun, who assisted Deena to the altar. She sat down and accepted the goblet, from which she drank deeply of the bitter, foul-smelling brew.

Almost instantly Deena was overcome by a wave of paralysis, which affected her entire body and she fell backwards onto the altar. She felt her consciousness being pushed out of the way by something, or someone, and then she heard a voice in her mind saying, "*Deena, I am your Peer. Grant me access to your body and mind. Grant me full access to your consciousness. Allow me to inter-penetrate your being and we shall become as one. And you shall have access to power beyond your wildest imaginings.*"

For a brief moment Deena thought of her clan and friends, of her Lemurian upbringing, of connection and belonging and community. And then she thought of the wealth and power and influence she would have by joining with Peer. She thought of how it would feel to have endless power; to never feel afraid or alone again and so she deliberately withdrew her consciousness and allowed the ingress of her new soul companion.

Deena felt her body begin to shiver and quake as alternating hot and cold flushes of perspiration ran down her body and her limbs began to thrash around with a life of their own. It felt as if her very soul was being torn apart to make room for the invading spirit. It felt as if she would never be able to survive the assault; as if she would shatter into a million little pieces and be scattered for ever. And then, suddenly, it was over.

Deena felt an immense wave of electric power run through her being. Suddenly she became aware of the thoughts and fears and concerns of every person in the room, at the same moment. What each had had for breakfast that morning... in fact what they had had for breakfast every morning of their lives. Who they secretly lusted after, their weaknesses, their hopes and dreams... Although she had always had access to her natural Lemurian telepathic abilities, these were now amplified beyond her wildest imaginings. She had access to almost infinite power, knowledge, insight...

"Ha ha haa!" Deena heard delighted laughter ringing through her mind. *"Oh no, this is simply too delicious!"* the voice continued. *"I see you! I see your story, Deena-who-is-Didu!"* With a gasp, Deena realised that this was the voice of her Peer, now speaking to her within her own mind, as her own thoughts. And she suddenly felt fear surging through her heart.

"Oh no, my sweet, do not fear. We are partnered now. I am yours and you are mine. I will not divulge our little secret! If anything, I am proud of the strength, fortitude and unique skills of my host. I will enable you to always screen this knowledge from any prying minds. We are going to achieve great things together, you and I. And, speaking of prying minds..."

"I told you, didn't I?" Enza's voice spoke in Didu's mind and she experienced a momentary terror, before realising that certain of her thoughts and knowledge were indeed screened from Enzu's mind. Didu found herself able to respond to Enza in the same way in which he had spoken to her, inside of his mind.

"*Yes, you did, but nothing could have prepared me for this! I can do anything, see anything and know anything. Anything at all!*"

As Deena accompanied Enza and the High Priest into the inner sanctum of the temple to receive their instructions for their new lives, she knew that the old Deena had indeed died that day, taking all vestiges of Didu with her, and that a new Deena had taken her place. There certainly was no turning back now...

The Green Lady had stopped speaking some time earlier. She sat, quietly staring into the undergrowth whilst I impatiently waited for her to recommence her story. Finally, I could wait no longer.

"*But, what happened next? You can't leave me hanging like that! Did Deena achieve her ambitions? Was she ever discovered to be a fraud? What happened to the Lemurian people? Did she ever see her clan again? Please, please finish the story!*"

The Green Lady looked up at me and smiled. "*Peter, please remember, it's just a story. You've become far too invested in our heroine's adventures!*

But yes, I can confirm that Deena did indeed, several years later, achieve the position of greatest power - that of High Priestess - and that she ruled for many years with Peer as her consort. Did she ever achieve true happiness or love? Did she ever see any of her family again? Unfortunately, not... to both questions. There was no way she could ever risk trying to see her clan again and she knew that they wouldn't have recognised her anyway, now that she was so irrevocably changed.

However, she enjoyed absolute control and had endless power and wealth, as well as luxury beyond her wildest imaginings. But she was also, at all times, burdened with conflicting emotions. She had a sense of derision for the Atlanteans, which was always underpinned by fear. She had truly conquered the conquerors and she knew that if they ever found out who she was or where she had come from, they would be deeply mortified; so much so that her life would be in danger. She had beaten them at their own game! But she had sold herself to accomplish this and there remained the constant fear of being discovered to be a fraud.

Then there was the contract with Peer, her psychic parasite. Although he gave her access to unlimited knowledge and power, he demanded a high price in return. Peer fed off lower frequency vibrations, such as fear and guilt and shame. Under his influence, Deena was drawn to participate in many depraved sexual activities, the abuse of alcohol and drugs, as well as in torture for pleasure and many other perversions of power. Peer thrived on the energies associated with these activities and, in return, provided Didu with ever more power and influence. She became immensely powerful, but remained deeply, deeply unhappy.

The Great Work of the Lemurian adepts paid off, and shortly after the events previously described, the entire Lemurian race achieved ascension and they disappeared completely from that plane of existence."

"But... does that mean that Deena would have left with them if she had made a different choice?"

"Yes indeed, Peter. But it was her destiny to experience a different path. And this is what she did."

"But... but it all seems rather unfair, doesn't it? I mean, Didu was only a child when she was kidnapped. What *choice did she really have? If she had revealed her true identity after the meteorite storm, she would probably just have landed up as a slave in a different household. She almost certainly would not have been able to make her way home to her clan. It feels to me as if the personality is a victim to the plans and contracts of the higher self."*

"Peter, remember that the personality <u>is</u> the higher self expressed into a specific reality. There is no separation between the two. Remember the hand in the glove? There are no victims here. The higher self chooses to have certain experiences in this place of forgetting in order to learn about who it truly is."

"So the higher self of Deena/Didu chose to have these experiences in order to learn about who and what it truly is? That is simply mind-boggling from the perspective of a human being incarnated on Earth at this time and place! But tell me, how did Deena's life end then?"

"There was another meteorite storm, many years later, when Deena was already an old woman and had been the ruling High Priestess for many years. The temple received a direct hit and she was killed almost immediately. This storm caused dramatic climactic and Earth changes, which annihilated the Atlantean civilisation. The few remaining people of this great civilisation were scattered all over the world, where they integrated with local primitive tribes."

"Wow, what an amazing story. But what does it all mean?"

"Well, that depends on the perspective from which you view the story. From one perspective it's just a rather improbable, mythic story about an early, lost civilisation. From another perspective, it's a story about the loss of self and the

ultimate betrayal of self. From another perspective, it's the soul history and the story of how I came to be."

She smiled quizzically at me and then stood, saying, *"That's enough for today, Peter. We will meet again next week when I will tell you a story about the ego's misguided search for love and acceptance."* And then, before I could say another word, the Green Lady drifted away and disappeared amongst the trees.

Gathering up my belongings, I realised that I felt completely exhausted and drained. The story told over the past two weeks had been an epic one and I was still no closer to finding out how this story had led to the Green Lady becoming the fascinating being that I had come to know.

I would spend considerable time in the following week transcribing and mulling over the stories that I had been told thus far. My fervent hope was that I would be able to make some sense out of these stories in order to reach some conclusions for myself as to the soul journey of the Green Lady.

CHAPTER 4:
EGO'S SEARCH FOR LOVE

The following week I arrived late at the forest clearing in a foul mood. I had written what I had thought to be an excellent article highlighting the challenges associated with managing the influx of tourists into Knysna for the annual oyster festival. There had been several recent reports of poor service and excessively long queues and I believed that I had made some excellent suggestions to address the problems at the end of my article. I had therefore been furious when the young, inexperienced features editor of a local rag had turned down my article with only a brief, dismissive note attached, saying, and I quote, "*Lacking substance and local knowledge*." The cheek of the little wench! I had been a top investigative journalist before she was even out of junior school!

In truth I was concerned, as several of my speculative pieces had recently been turned down. I just couldn't understand it. I had thought that the community of Knysna and the surrounding towns should consider themselves fortunate to have a journalist of my calibre in residence and that it would be a simple matter to write sufficient articles to support myself financially. I had to admit to myself that my ego was bruised.

The Green Lady was seated on her customary log when I burst into the clearing. With a mumbled apology I flung myself down onto the ground and rummaged my pen and notebook out of my rucksack. I sat with my pen poised above the paper for a long while, waiting for her to begin speaking. When there was no sound from her, I looked up enquiringly. Her emerald-green eyes were filled with merriment, and some small measure of pity.

"*And so, exactly on time, the objections arise,*" she murmured.

"*Objections? What do you mean?*" I asked, feeling somewhat confused and rather defensive.

"*Whenever we decide to have the courage to follow our hearts instead of our egos, there is an initial period of euphoria, immediately followed by a whole host of objections arising. It's absolutely inevitable. The ego hates change and it hates not being in charge. It is just waiting to point out the reasons why all of this has been a very bad idea and why you should immediately go back to what you know: the ego running the show. It is exactly now when you need to dig even deeper into your reserves of courage and fortitude. Exactly now when you need to keep returning to your heart connection and trusting that all is proceeding exactly as it should. And, believe me, it absolutely is proceeding perfectly.*"

"*But... I'm not so sure,*" I admitted, feeling my irritation dissolving in the face of her kindness and empathy. "*I mean, I thought I could support a modest lifestyle on the income I could generate by writing articles for local publications. It should be so easy for an experienced journalist such as myself. For heaven's sake, I should be able to do this in my sleep! But my articles keep getting turned down and I'm running through my savings at an alarming rate. Perhaps this wasn't such a good idea after all. Perhaps I'm going to have to return to the city with my tail between my legs and beg for my old job back!*" I dropped my head into my hands and wallowed for a good minute or two in self-pity before I felt a light touch on my arm. I looked up into my companion's sympathetic, smiling eyes.

"*Peter, you are asking of yourself to stretch; to find a new way of being that is very different from the way that has always worked for you in the past. And, of course, it's not comfortable or easy to find a new way of being. The temptation is huge to revert to what you have always done. But I would like to remind you that you decided to find another way of being exactly because the old way wasn't actually working for you, was it? You were feeling as if your life had no meaning or purpose. You were running yourself ragged doing a job in the city that didn't fulfil you any more. The reality is that you can't actually go back, Peter. You truly cannot cross the same river twice. You are no longer the person that you were. You have to move forward, my friend.*"

"*OK, OK, I know that you're right. But... I don't know what I'm going to do if I can't support myself with my writing. That's all I know how to do. I'm going to have to find another solution and I have absolutely no idea of what that could be...*"

"*Peter, let me remind you of what catalysed this life change in the first place. You started to listen to your heart; you put your heart in the driver's seat instead of your ego. That is what brought you to this moment, right now. So, it doesn't make sense to revert now, at this late stage, to the ego being in the driver's seat, does it? Close your eyes now... just breathe... breathe and feel your physical heart beating.*"

I did what the Green Lady bade me to do and, for a minute or two, I simply sat quietly and listened to my heart beating. Gradually I felt myself calming down and my fears and anger began to subside. I started to become aware of the birds singing and of the sighing of the breeze in the treetops. The sunlight warmed my cheek and suddenly I found an unexpected joy stealing through my being. This life was still exactly what I wanted! I wanted to have the freedom and time and space to live in this beautiful, peaceful part of the world, without the commitment and pressure of city living and a big, stressful job. I sighed deeply with contentment and allowed my mind to float.

Within a very short while, a great idea for a new story sidled up and began to tentatively nudge at the corners of my mind. My eyes flew open and I grabbed my pen and notebook to quickly jot the idea down. Then I somewhat sheepishly looked up at the Green Lady.

"I'm sorry. I guess I just forgot for a moment that you were here. I don't mean to waste your time. I'm also sorry that I was so grumpy when I arrived. I'm ready to start on today's story now."

"It's perfectly fine, Peter. Sometimes we all need a little reminder to go to our hearts to re-connect with who we really are. This world can be a very challenging place and it's really easy to forget ourselves and to fall prey to our fears. Your heart is your direct portal to your higher self. Just stay in your heart, as far as possible, and all will be well. You are on your path; don't ever doubt that.

It is, however, an interesting co-incidence that you are struggling with your ego at the moment, because our next story is all about ego and about what happens when we allow a rampant ego to run the show. So, let's get started then, shall we?"

Jean-Philippe could hear Marthe softly, almost inaudibly, murmuring to Marie-Claire as she bustled around cleaning up the room after having helped the little girl to dress. Every single word of Marie-Claire's high-pitched, excited chattering was, by contrast, quite audible to the boy hidden in the alcove behind the woven wall hanging just outside the door. His upper lip curled in a dismissive sneer at the constant stream of inanities that flowed, seemingly unchecked, from her lips. Girls were so pathetic and boring and, although he had only met her for the first time two days earlier, he believed his little cousin to be far worse than most. The chattering hadn't stopped since his father's sister, his aunt Clarice, her husband, Reynaud, and their little daughter had arrived earlier that week. And, unbelievably, the grown-ups appeared to find the brat enchanting and amusing! But even worse was the fact that the little slip of a girl had actually had the audacity to snub him when her family and their entourage had arrived for their intended two-week stay.

"This is your cousin, Jean-Philippe, little pumpkin," his aunt had said and the boy had reached out to take his cousin's hand as he had been taught by his tutor. But, before he could raise her hand to his lips, his older brother, Claude, had appeared in the doorway to his left. Marie-Claire's mouth had fallen open in astonishment and admiration and she had forgotten all about Jean-Philippe.

Claude was fourteen, tall, dark-haired and handsome and every single girl he met fell in love with him on the spot. Jean-Philippe had ground his teeth in fury and embarrassment as his cousin had turned her back on him and presented her hand to Claude, fluttering her long, dark eyelashes as she dropped into a simpering little curtsey.

"What a pleasure to meet my lovely cousin! Come, let me show you the puppies in the stable," said Claude, with his usual easy charm, and Marie-Claire had followed after him with a look of melting adoration in her eyes. The adults had moved on, leaving Jean-Philippe standing, seething with jealousy, rage and humiliation in the hallway.

"I'll teach that little bitch a lesson she'll never forget!" he vowed to himself with clenched fists, his nails digging into the palms of his hands. This particular mix of emotions was very familiar to the boy, as his older brother had always been everyone's favourite. Even Jean-Philippe himself couldn't help liking and admiring his perfect older brother, who had always treated him with an off-hand, careless sort of affability. He couldn't hate his brother, but he hated the fact that everything was so easy for Claude and that their father simply didn't appear to care as much for his younger son as he did for the elder.

Jean-Philippe knew that his elder brother would inherit all of their father's considerable wealth and many properties and that Claude was already being trained and groomed to take over the running of their father's business interests. Jean-Philippe, on the other hand, showed neither aptitude nor interest in being involved in managing the vast textile manufacturing and farming concerns, nor being involved in the powerful local political organisations active in the South of France at the time. He didn't excel at his lessons with the boys' private tutor, as did Claude, and he knew that his position as second son would mean that he would probably end up serving either in the military or in the clergy. Heaven forbid that the latter should occur!

Actually Jean-Philippe had always dreamed of being a dashing Grenadier in the heavy cavalry, striking fear into the hearts of the enemy as he led the charge into battle. He would spend hours arranging his tin soldiers in battle formations, depicting famous skirmishes between the allied forces of Prussia, Austria and Germany against the French, under the leadership of Generale Dumouriez, who was his current hero.

Jean-Philippe was probably well-suited to serving in the military, as the boy was a natural-born fighter. He liked nothing better than to pick fights with other boys; fights which he invariably won, due to his physical courage as well as his height and strength advantage over other boys of his age. Although his father and his tutor often beat him for getting involved in scraps with the local boys, Jean-Philippe believed that one day he would be decorated with medals honouring his courage on the battlefield and that his father would finally be proud of him for his fighting abilities.

The boys' mother had died of a fever within days of bringing Jean-Philippe into the world and this could have been the reason why his father resented the boy. The only time he paid Jean-Philippe any attention at all was when he was beating him for some infraction or another. For the rest of the time, his focus was solely on the grooming of his elder son as his successor.

Jean-Philippe again clenched his fists in anger at the thought of his father's regular dismissal of him and he burned with the desire to inflict his own pain upon another. Just then, the door to Marie-Claire's room opened and Marthe exited, calling over her shoulder to her young charge, "*Sit quietly now and work on your primer until I return. Don't get your dress rumpled or dirty or your mother will be very angry with you. You need to look like a young lady for our luncheon with your cousins and uncle.*"

Jean-Philippe, peering out from behind the wall hanging, waited until Marthe's dark skirts disappeared around the corner before cautiously turning the doorknob and entering the room, silently pulling the door closed behind him. Marie-Claire was sitting primly upright on a chaise-lounge, resentfully stabbing her needle into the rather grubby fabric stretched taut in an embroidery frame on her lap. She looked up as Jean-Philippe entered the room and her eyes widened with shock.

"What... what are you doing here? Boys aren't allowed into girls' rooms, you know. Maman would be very angry. You'd better leave now!" Her voice quavered on the last sentence as she observed an alarming glint in Jean-Philippe's eyes. Some basic instinct for self-preservation caused the little girl to leap to her feet, her embroidery tumbling unheeded to the floor. She started backing away from her cousin, her eyes hypnotically fixed upon those of the older boy.

In two rapid steps, Jean-Philippe covered the distance between them and grabbed her arm, pulling Marie-Claire close to him and fiercely whispering into her ear, *"Little bitch, I'm going to show you a thing or two today. You'll discover who's actually in charge in this place! Let me give you a hint - it's not your precious Claude!"* Marie-Claire gasped with terror and yanked her arm out of her cousin's grasp. As he was blocking her exit via the door, she turned and ran in the opposite direction - towards the canopied bed in the corner of the room. She jumped onto the bed and pulled the drapes around herself for protection.

"Perfect!" Jean-Philippe whispered to himself and slowly smiled as he casually sauntered over to the bed where his cousin was crouched, now sobbing with fear. He jerked the

drapes out of her grasp and knelt on the bed, smiling with glee, as he felt himself becoming aroused. This was an occurrence which had recently become quite frequent and one of which he was rapidly becoming overly fond. *"You can't escape me, you stupid girl. I'm going to do just exactly as I please with you. And, if you tell anyone, I'll come back and kill you!"*

A terrified Marie-Claire furiously kicked backwards away from her cousin in a froth of white petticoats, her red, tear-stained face contorted with fear. Jean-Philippe grabbed both her legs and pulled her towards him, her skirts and petticoats bunching up around her waist. The little girl began screaming and so Jean-Philippe clamped a hand over her mouth to silence her and used his knee to pin her body to the bed. He pinched her hard on the soft underside of her arm and then, rising up, removed his hand from her mouth and slapped her hard across her face three or four times before clamping her mouth shut again. The little girl's eyes rolled back in her head with shock and terror. Holding her neck down with his elbow, he began to explore beneath her petticoats. He could feel her soft, smooth, chubby thighs and his hand moved ever higher as his excitement grew to fever pitch. This was so much better than he had ever imagined it would be!

Just then, Marthe's voice called out in the distance and Marie-Claire took advantage of the moment of distraction to kick Jean-Philippe hard in the groin and to roll off the bed and run to the door, screaming for the servant all the while. Cursing with pain and frustration, Jean-Philippe jumped off the bed, hobbled to the door and made his escape. That damned brat! He'd have to find another opportunity to further his explorations.

But this was not to be. Despite her cousin's threats, Marie-Claire told Marthe exactly what had happened, and Marthe duly reported the entire story to her mistress. The family cut their visit short and departed within the hour.

Jean-Philippe was summoned to his father's study where he was given the beating of his life with his father's walking cane. But the expression of utter disgust and disappointment on his father's face was far worse than the beating. This expression was to haunt Jean-Philippe for the rest of his days because it was to be the last time that he ever saw his father. After being banished to his room in solitary confinement with only bread and water for a whole two weeks, Jean Philippe was informed by his tutor that he would be leaving for military boarding school the following day. As the coach departed, Jean-Philippe craned his neck, still hoping to catch a glimpse of his father, but he was doomed to disappointment. His father remained in his study, still too angry to even bid his younger son farewell.

During his two years in boarding school, the only visitor that Jean-Philippe ever had was his brother Claude, who informed him that their father had issued orders that Jean-Philippe would not be welcomed home for the holidays. At fifteen, Jean-Philippe was transferred to the École Militaire, the military academy in Paris, from which he graduated two years later. This was the same prestigious academy from which Napoleon had graduated in 1785, fourteen years earlier. Jean-Philippe spent the holiday after graduation with a friend, deciding, out of spite, not to inform anyone of his whereabouts. By the time he returned home two months later, he discovered that his father had passed away after breaking his neck during a serious horse riding accident. Jean-Philippe's father had been buried without his younger son's knowledge, as the family had been unable to trace the young man to give him the news. As expected, the family business now resided in the capable hands of Claude-the-perfect.

Jean-Philippe's father had, however, made provision for his younger son in the form of a minor country estate and a small annual stipend. This stipend would prove to be sufficient for Jean-Philippe to purchase the necessary uniforms and horses to follow his dream of gaining a commission in the military.

Jean-Philippe had excelled in both horsemanship and swordsmanship at the military academy and had gained a reputation for fearlessness, both of which, in addition to meeting the height requirements, enabled him to achieve an appointment as a second Lieutenant in Napoleon's Cuirassiers.

Between graduating from the military academy and joining Napoleon's army, Jean-Philippe spent a few months at his inherited property in the south of France. For most of this time, despite the hunting and fishing, the distraction of village girls and practising his horsemanship and sword fighting skills, Jean-Philippe was bored out of his mind.

One morning, the curator of his estate reported to him that a poacher had been caught setting traps in the small wood on the western border of his property. Although he drew his brows together in a frown, Jean-Philippe was secretly elated. At last, something to do! He instructed his men to bound the poacher with ropes in the window-less stone storage room beneath the kitchens. Then he gave them tasks to complete that would keep them far away from the house. He dismissed the kitchen staff for the day, as he would not require any witnesses for the delights that lay ahead. As Jean-Philippe descended the cold, torch-lit stairs to the cellar, he found himself eagerly anticipating the upcoming few hours.

Upon entering the room he found the poacher sitting on a wooden chair, with his hands tied to the chair behind his back and his feet tied to the legs of the chair.

"Monsieur, I'm sorry... I didn't mean to... I'll never do it again, I swear," the man stammered, his forehead beaded with sweat and his eyes widening in alarm to witness the sneering face and the excitement flickering in the eyes of his captor. The man was dressed in leather breeches and had been stripped to the waist, as requested by Jean-Philippe. Despite the cold room, he was drenched in perspiration and had an ugly cut above one eye, his torso covered in welts and bruises. Clearly he had put up a fight upon being apprehended by Jean-Philippe's men. Jean-Philippe's nostrils widened as he caught the unmistakeable metallic scent of fear and he found himself becoming aroused. This was going to be really entertaining...

"Please, Monsieur, it... it was for my family. We're starving..." the man's words were cut short as Jean-Philippe delivered two stinging blows to his cheeks with the back of his hand. Then he pulled an old, dirty rag that he had brought with him for this purpose out of his pocket, wadded it up and stuffed it into the man's mouth. He secured the rag in place with a rope that he tied so tight that the man's mouth was pulled back in a grimace. The poacher's eyes rolled in terror and the reek of sweat and fear intensified in the cold room. Jean-Philippe pulled the sharp kitchen knife he had brought

with him from the pocket of his cloak and tested the blade with his thumb. Then he slowly looked into the horrified eyes of his plaything and gleefully smiled. For the first time in months he was no longer bored. He was going to have some real fun today...

Jean-Philippe commenced his military career in April 1800 as a 2nd Lieutenant in the heavy cavalry of the then First Consul of France, Napoleon Bonaparte. In fulfilment of his childhood dream, he was appointed to the Cuirassiers, the true descendants of the medieval knights. These were large men mounted on big, heavy horses, who were used for shock tactics on the battlefield; moving in close formation in a massive, irresistible charge. Jean-Philippe wore with pride the uniform of the 3rd Cuirassier regiment of deep-blue coat with red collar and turn backs, buff trousers, body armour called the cuirass, and helmet. His height, combined with his dashing black moustache and his imposing uniform, meant that he was never short of attention from the ladies. Or, indeed, from the whores who followed the armies on their campaigns. But, far more importantly, he excelled on the battlefield as well.

Showing extreme courage and superior swordsmanship during the Battle of Hohenlinden in December 1800, Jean-Philippe was rapidly promoted to 1st Lieutenant. His talents were put to good use over the next few years, including during the Ulm campaign and in the defeat of the Austrians and Russians during the Battle of Austerlitz. When his commanding officer was killed during the Battle of Jena-Auerstedt, Jean-Philippe was promoted to Captain in the 1st regiment of the reserve cavalry in Napoleon's Grande Armée.

Jean-Philippe now dreamed of becoming a member of the Imperial Guard's Horse Grenadiers, the elite force of heavy cavalry, nicknamed The Gods, and recognisable by their distinctive bearskin headwear and massive black horses. He had every hope of this dream being fulfilled as he was being noticed by some very influential people. Jean-Philippe knew that progression through the ranks of Napoleon's army was based on merit, rather than on birth, breeding or access to financial resources, as it was in the other European armies of the time. Even though Jean-Philippe was, at this point, only twenty-five years old, he already had a well-deserved reputation for being fiercely courageous and unstoppable on the battlefield. He required only another few years of experience and a couple of citations for bravery before he would become eligible for selection into this elite Guard.

In January 1807, Jean-Philippe's squadron was settled into winter quarters just outside of Warsaw. Napoleon, who was by now Emperor of France, had ordered his army to be stationed in-and-around Poland to recover and to refit for upcoming campaigns after destroying the Prussian army and chasing the Russians into Poland. In severe snow and below-freezing temperatures, the commanders received word of a surprise attack planned by the Russians, hoping to defeat the scattered French armies. Napoleon ordered a concentration of his army and the chase was on after the Russians, despite the terrible weather conditions.

Just outside the small Polish town of Preussich-Eylau, the Russians turned to face the pursuing French, with some confidence, as they outnumbered them by sixty-seven thousand men to forty-nine thousand, and had almost double the artillery pieces. Jean-Philippe's squadron, as part of Marshall Murat's reserve cavalry, were amongst the first to arrive on the plateau a mile outside of the town, but they would have to wait for the following day to see any real action.

Early the following morning, despite heavy snowfalls, an exchange of artillery fire was followed by a French infantry assault of the Russian line, which was easily repulsed. The Russian army, now greatly emboldened, advanced against the French line, which showed signs of breaking altogether. After more than three hours of battle, Napoleon's position was grim indeed, and he decided to call in his reserve cavalry and also the cavalry of his Imperial Guard. Napoleon commanded Murat to charge the centre of the Russian line.

Upon receiving the command, Jean-Philippe began lining up his company behind the shattered French centre line, along with the rest of the over ten-thousand strong French cavalry. As the senior Captain, he would lead the charge of both his own company and the second company of his squadron. The Russian infantry, formed in three lines with a battery of almost seventy guns, lay two-and-a-half thousand yards ahead. This was an extremely long cavalry charge and Jean-Philippe knew that his men and their horses would be tested to their very limit.

At the order, the massive body of French horsemen began their long charge, stepping out into the driving snow, their long, straight-bladed sabres held level in front of them, their bodies leaning forward into the motion of their horses.

Eighty squadrons of French cavalry began charging the Russian line. Jean-Philippe's heart pounded in his chest with excitement. He felt powerful; unstoppable! The thundering hoof beats of over ten thousand horses reverberated throughout his entire body; the driving snow stung his eyes and the clouds of acrid smoke from the recent infantry action reduced visibility to virtually zero. Jean-Philippe didn't care. His instincts had taken over. This was what he had been born to do!

And then, suddenly, they were upon the columns of Russian infantry marching on Eylau. The infantry parted before the irresistible force of the heavy cavalry like ripe wheat before a scythe; and like wheat were levelled to the ground. Breaking this first Russian line, Jean-Philippe led his men into the flank of Russian cavalry, which had been supporting the infantry attack, and cut them to pieces, before driving on towards the main Russian lines. The cavalry charge overran and disabled much of the lethal Russian artillery as they went, and broke both the remaining Russian lines. Jean-Philippe observed with considerable satisfaction the French Imperial Guard breaking the Russian cavalry reserve. He knew that one day, very soon, he too would be riding with The Gods!

Then he wheeled his horse around in preparation to lead his exhausted men into a single cavalry column, to charge back through the line of Russian infantry and artillery batteries, which had subsequently re-formed. Murat's command was for the cavalry to regroup behind the French centre line.

On the charge back to the French line, Jean-Philippe encountered a Horse Grenadier of the Russian Reserve, twenty paces ahead, blocking his way. He charged straight for the man, his sword held steady and level, despite his exhaustion. As the horses passed each other, Jean-Philippe felt the Russian's sword penetrating his right shoulder, at the very edge of his cuirass. His sabre went flying out of his hand and the force of the blow knocked him right off his horse.

Jean-Philippe landed on his back, winded, as his horse galloped on without him. Jumping to his feet only seconds later, his right arm dangling uselessly, he searched frantically for his sabre, as he noticed out of the corner of his eye the imminent approach of a Russian soldier bearing a curved sabre. Jean-Philippe kicked the smaller man's feet out from under him and delivered another sharp kick to his opponent's face, relishing the satisfying crunch of the man's nose breaking as he fell backwards, relinquishing his sabre. In one rapid movement, Jean-Philippe grabbed the sabre from the ground with his unwounded left hand and slashed at his attacker's neck; the arterial spray from the wound assuring him that the threat was neutralised.

As Jean-Philippe continued to anxiously search for his horse and his own sabre, he fought off two more attackers with his enemy's sword before hearing a familiar, loud whinnying right behind him. He whipped around, only to be confronted by the dismaying sight of his horse rearing up; his massive hooves descending as Jean-Philippe stumbled over one of his slain enemies and fell backwards onto the ground.

His last conscious thought before the horse's front left hoof crushed his chest was of his father. Jean-Philippe died, filled with rage at the ignobility of his death and burning regret that his father would never be proud of him now...

CHAPTER 5:
DEPENDENCY ON THE
OTHER

On the following Sunday I arrived at the clearing in the forest in a state of considerable excitement. The story that the Green Lady had shared the previous week had really fired my imagination and I had spent the week doing research on the role of the heavy cavalry in the Napoleonic campaigns. My dreams during the past week had been filled with glorious, triumphant battlefield scenes and I often awoke to the faint, lingering scents of cordite and sweat, horse manure and blood, with the dying screams of my enemies, musket fire and the terrified whinnying of horses ringing in my ears.

Although I understood that Jean-Philippe had died what he obviously considered to be an ignoble death by being killed by his own horse on the battlefield, still I felt a great deal of respect and admiration for his abilities as a soldier. However, his personality, not to mention his questionable ethics as a man, I found to be far less admirable.

Settling down in my customary spot, nestled amongst the roots of the giant Yellowwood tree, I leant my head back against the trunk, closed my eyes and gave myself over to vivid battle scenes of glory and honour.

"*It is true that warfare allows for experiences of unparalleled intensity. These experiences truly do foster great learning about the nature of ones own being, and also that of ones fellow man.*"

I opened my eyes to find the Green Lady sitting on her customary moss-covered log and smiling at me.

"*Warfare also allows for the full expression of the ego, and the subsequent fall-out provides great opportunities for exploring a different way of being.*"

"*I'm not sure I understand what you mean by that,*" I admitted, sitting upright with my pen poised above a new page in my notebook.

"*The soul chooses to incarnate into many different life situations, time periods and challenges in order to experience the full complement of growth and learning opportunities available in this reality. From the perspective of the higher self, none of those experiences are either good or bad - they are merely the background story that provides the context for the pre-agreed learning of a particular lifetime.*

In the case of the soldier, Jean-Philippe, he chose to experience an early life of privilege, luxury and parental neglect in order to proceed even further down the path of excessive ego, the door to which had been opened in the lifetime as Deena. Full ego expression and complete capitulation to hyper-masculine traits would allow the full experience of what would happen under those circumstances. Then, as an officer in the well-renowned and highly regarded Cuirassiers de Cheval, followed by numerous battle successes, his ego was polished to a high gloss. And his ignoble death promoted the learning that all ego accomplishments are as nothing and must surely come to naught upon the death of the personality."

"*But, surely Jean-Philippe also had some good traits? He was incredibly brave and loyal to his men and to his comrades. He was a natural leader, strong and dependable and powerful,*" I commented.

"*But, of course! He developed all of the masculine traits to their fullest extent and there can be no judgment of that. In fact, ultimately, there is no good or bad; only that which takes us further into separation - into the game - and that which takes us out of separation and closer to our own higher selves. All souls heading into the deepest forgetting of separation will eventually turn around and make their way back to Oneness. It is all just an elaborate game. But, in the playing of the game, we learn about ourselves. We see ourselves in the mirror of the other and in the mirror of the world around us. And, in the end, it's all just stories within stories,*" said the Green Lady.

"*I must say, I was rather surprised to be told a story about a male lifetime after the previous story about the female, Didu. Somehow, I had thought that a being would always incarnate as either a male or as a female, but not both. It's quite strange for me to consider that I might have had lifetimes as a woman!*"

"*You most certainly have had lifetimes as a woman, Peter. The spirit has no gender, of course. But, in order to truly explore this system, it's important for beings to experience many different perspectives; one of which is the issue of gender.*"

"*So, as an aggressively masculine man, Jean-Philippe was able to have some important experiences, which allowed him to begin to see himself in a new light? Would he choose different experiences in his next lifetime, I wonder?*"

"Well, yes. But not as Jean-Philippe, of course. Jean-Philippe was merely a personality, like a set of clothing that the higher self can put on and take off. He was a set of experiences which allowed the indwelling spirit to learn about itself. And yes, a very different set of life experiences would be chosen for the next lifetime. In fact, that's what I'm going to tell you about today.

This next lifetime would be about finding some connection with another, but not in a healthy way. It would be about attempting to find salvation in another, when it can only truly be found in oneself. This is the lifetime of David Sinclair..."

What was to be, in hindsight, the defining moment of David Sinclair's life, arrived unexpectedly at the very end of a long week that didn't start out well at all. In fact, the week began rather horribly on Monday morning with a very loud pounding at David's front door. David awoke with a start and then groaned as the pounding continued; now matched, in a syncopated rhythm, by an equally loud pounding in his head. Picking up his timepiece from the table at his bedside, he cursed aloud to notice that it was after eleven am.

In what had proved to be a futile attempt to call up his muse, David had finished three bottles of wine the previous night and could not recall getting into bed at all. The pounding in his head was now further exacerbated by a spiking pain in his eyeballs and David rolled over onto his stomach and covered his head with a pillow, as he continued to softly moan to himself.

But the pillow could not muffle the ever-increasing volume of the knocking and pounding at his door. *"Arnold, please answer the door,"* David managed, at barely more than a whisper, but then belatedly recalled that dear old Pater had stopped paying Arnold's salary a couple of months earlier and that Arnold had subsequently left David's employ.

"Open the door, David. Young man, I know you're in there. Open this door, right this minute!" David recognised the familiar strident and peremptory tones of his father's voice and cursed softly at the realisation of the inevitable unpleasantness of the forthcoming, unscheduled meeting.

Muttering beneath his breath, David dragged himself upright into a seated position and cradled his head in his hands as he waited for the wave of nausea to pass. Then he gingerly got to his feet, pulled on his robe and unsteadily shuffled over to the door. He was well aware that it wouldn't do to antagonise his father any further. Without the allowance that his parents paid him, David would rapidly find himself out on the streets. He knew too that most of his friends had, at this point, already given up on him.

David pulled open the door, to find his father impeccably turned out, as usual, in morning dress, with his cane raised in preparation to knock once more at the door.

"David, this is simply disgraceful!" James Sinclair expostulated as he pushed his way past David to assume his normal stance of rigid parental disapproval in front of the mantelpiece. *"It's past eleven and I find you still a-bed! For the love of God, boy! When are you ever going to make anything of your life? How do you expect me to believe that you'll ever make your living as an artist if you hardly ever produce a single painting? And those that you do produce are simply not worth selling! I'm telling you, my boy, if it weren't for the intercession of your doting Mother on your behalf, I would have cut you off without a penny a long time ago!"*

Sighing, David threw himself into a wingback chair and allowed the familiar tirade to wash over his head. He had endured the selfsame lecture a hundred times before, ever since he had graduated from Eton three years earlier. In fact, his entire life had taken place against the gloomy backdrop of his father's disappointment in him. He was also aware that his father's threats were meaningless, as his mother controlled the purse strings and he had always been her favourite. Not for the first time, David thanked his lucky stars that his elder brother, Reginald, was such a dutiful son and had so willingly followed in their father's footsteps. Reginald was now a barrister in their father's legal firm and doing him proud every single day, no doubt. David choked down the familiar bitterness of envy and resentment in his throat. But, he reflected, at least with Reginald doing his familial duty, there had been a modicum of freedom for David to follow his own interests during the past few years.

David's father, James Sinclair, had himself been a lowly legal clerk when he had first met Catherine Margaret Wallace, the only child of wealthy industrialist, Stanley Wallace. Mr Wallace had engaged the services of Bertram, Bertram and Henley, the legal firm for which James Sinclair had been working at the time, to manage a property deal for him. Stanley Wallace was to regret ever after his decision to have his beloved daughter meet him that day at the legal firm so that he could take her out for lunch after his legal briefing had been concluded.

Catherine arrived early and was shown to the small library and supplied with a cup of tea by the receptionist. It was here that she first laid eyes upon young James Sinclair, who was doing research for a case that one of the partners was working on. Catherine who, at eighteen, had already been introduced to numerous potential husbands by her father and had found every single one of them lacking in some way, fell head-over-heels in love with the handsome young clerk. There was just something about his shy smile and his quiet, unassuming demeanour that touched her heart in a way that none of the wealthy, successful men her father deemed to be suitable husband material, did.

Needless to say, Catherine's father had denounced as preposterous James Sinclair's stammering request to court his daughter and had thenceforth forbidden Catherine to ever see James again. But Catherine was her father's daughter and she was possessed of a deeply stubborn streak. She had never been denied anything in her short, spoiled life and her father's denial of James's request made her even more determined to have James for her husband. Just like any general going into battle, she knew her enemy well and she cleverly made a strategic decision to attack Stanley in the one place in which he was weakest; his deep love for his daughter.

Catherine went on a hunger strike, making it very clear that she would refuse to eat until Stanley agreed that she could marry James. Stanley, watching his beloved lovely, young daughter fading away and becoming a wraith before his very eyes, eventually gave in and the two young people were married shortly after Catherine's nineteenth birthday. Stanley used several of his contacts and provided the wherewithal for James to rapidly be trained as a barrister and thereafter to be appointed as a partner into a prestigious law firm. At least, Stanley conceded, the young man had a promising future and seemed intelligent and driven.

However, on one point Stanley refused to compromise: he would not allow James to control his daughter's fortune. In 1882, just twenty years earlier, the Married Women's Property Act had ensured a wife's right to own, buy and sell her separate property. Stanley Wallace was therefore able to ensure that James would not be able to lay a hand on Catherine's money or several properties and businesses. Upon her marriage, he settled a rather generous annual stipend upon his daughter and, when he died ten years later, Catherine became the sole inheritor of his considerable wealth, including the mansion in which the family currently lived. James was not able to touch a penny of Catherine's money and this was to become the source of much resentment to him.

Although James earned a good wage as a barrister, Catherine was the one holding the real wealth and she was astute enough not to concede any of this power to her husband. Catherine decided when and where and how her money was spent and she kept James on a tight leash. Catherine was an intelligent woman and, together with the managers she appointed to direct her father's business interests, her inheritance continued to grow at a steady pace.

The one area in which Catherine and James disagreed most heatedly about the expenditure of her money was on her younger son. Whereas Reginald was James's favourite, David had always been the apple of his mother's eye. From young she had recognised and encouraged his artistic talent and it was she who had provided him with the best tutors, art supplies and, later, had paid for his tuition with an up-and-coming young painter in France. David had thoroughly enjoyed his three year sojourn in Paris, but had returned to

London seemingly without any ambitions of making a living out of his considerable talent and many opportunities.

After another six months of drinking, gambling and womanising, even David's indulgent mother was starting to lose patience with her younger son. Despite having been given every advantage and the financial wherewithal to practice his art, it seemed as if he would never amount to much. Catherine had persuaded several of her influential friends to commission paintings from her son, but David had always lost interest in the works depicting their spoilt, chubby children and tedious pets and had, to date, not completed a single one of his commissions. This was quite an embarrassment for Catherine and she was finally tiring of making excuses for her feckless son. Catherine was her father's daughter and even she now realised that she would have to pull in the reins and strongly encourage her son to commit to something, least she be saddled with an overgrown man-child hanging onto her apron strings for the rest of her life.

And so it was, with great reluctance that Catherine conceded to her husband's demands that they begin to reduce David's allowance in an attempt to force him to grow up. The first casualty in this battle of attrition was David's manservant, Arnold. Catherine had given James permission to stop payment of the servant's salary; a task that he had gladly carried out. David now had only the part-time services of a single maid to take care of his basic cooking, cleaning and laundry.

But, alas, the loss of his manservant had not encouraged David to grow up at all. If anything, he seemed to sink still further into his life of debauchery. He actually became an even greater source of embarrassment to his parents as, without his manservant to keep him looking like a gentleman, David was now often seen around town wearing dirty, stained and crumpled clothing. Catherine realised that something drastic would have to be done.

After much discussion and debate and tears and recriminations, Catherine and James had finally decided that they would give David an ultimatum: either shape up and start earning some money, or he would lose the use of his apartment. He had until the end of the year, after which he would have to begin paying rent. Furthermore, he would be disinherited too. Of course, Catherine had no intention of carrying out that particular threat, but this information she did not share with her husband. James was deputised to inform David of his parents' decision because Catherine could not bear to carry out this unpleasant task herself.

It was, therefore, with great glee that James donned his top hat, best buff waistcoat and long, black coat that morning. Finally, his son would be forced to become a man and to stop embarrassing his parents with his wastrel ways.

Gradually the realisation dawned upon David that there was a different tone to his father's familiar lecture. Looking up, he was surprised to catch a fleeting gleeful glint in his father's eye and it was then that he knew that his days of freedom and minimal responsibility were coming to an end. For once, David sat up straight, looked his father straight in the eye and actually listened. There might be a way to turn this situation to his advantage if he paid attention now.

"And so, David, our terms are as follows: you have until the end of December, six months from now, to finally prove to us that you can make a living out of your painting. After the end of December, you will have to pay the rent on this apartment by yourself and will no longer receive any

financial support from your mother and myself. If you are unable to afford to take care of yourself at that point, then you will have one of two choices: to either accept a position within one of your mother's companies, to which we will appoint you, or be left to rot on your own. And if you don't perform according to our requirements in this position, your services will be terminated and, again, you will be left to fend for yourself. That's it, no more financial support. You don't know how lucky you are, my boy. If I'd had my way, I'd have cut you off long ago. Why, when I was your age..."

David recognised that his father's monologue had now strayed back into familiar territory and so he tuned out the droning voice and tried to focus his fuzzy mind on the situation at hand. He realised that he was now in quite a predicament. Unbeknownst to his parents, he had racked up considerable gambling debts and, despite the extremely generous annual stipend he had, until now, been receiving, he was already in a rather precarious situation. Now, with the additional threat of having all financial support removed, he realised that he'd have to finally start making his own way in the world.

With a small, inward sigh of regret, David accepted his lot and decided to get on with it. It had been a wonderful life whilst it had lasted, but all good things eventually came to an end and he knew that he now needed to demonstrate at least some willing to his parents. He had no doubt that a few small concessions on his part would probably be enough to regain his mother's support, both emotionally and financially, and so he decided to set his mind to accomplishing just that.

Once his father had finally departed, with many additional warnings and exhortations to change his ways,

David splashed water on his face, dressed and ate breakfast in preparation to finding a solution to his many problems.

David was well aware of the fact that he had more than enough talent and ability, and so he decided to complete a few paintings which he would sell before the end of the year in order to demonstrate his willingness to change. He had been approached a year earlier by an art dealer who had seen a few of the smaller paintings that David had completed whilst in Paris. After purchasing the small stock of paintings, the dealer had indicated that he would be willing to purchase any new work that David could produce. So this then would be David's rescue plan. He had no doubt whatsoever that he would be able to pay his own way once his six months of grace were over.

But, by the end of the following week, which David had spent staring for hours on end at the pristine blank canvas on the easel before him; he was no longer so sure. Whilst in Paris, he had had no difficulty in producing one painting after another; many of which had been declared to be reasonable by his teacher and magnificent by his fellow students. But now, it seemed, his muse had completely abandoned him. His mind seemed empty of ideas; his paintbrush felt as heavy as lead and the colours on his palette all appeared garish, strident and incapable of portraying anything with subtlety.

David threw down his paintbrush and flung himself into his chair, closing his eyes and leaning his head against the headrest. For the first time ever in his life, he felt unsure of himself and worried about his future. If his talent had deserted him, then what was he? He'd have to work in some menial, soul-destroying, lowly position in one of his mother's companies. That, or be cast out onto the street.

All David had ever wanted to do was paint. He wanted to produce great works of art, such as he had gazed at in admiration for hours in the galleries in Europe. His secret fear was that he would never produce anything worthwhile. That he would produce ordinary, boring, merely competent portraits that would be purchased by ordinary, boring people and that he would never reach the heights attained by the artists he so admired. It was simply easier not to try at all than to risk mediocrity.

David's wallow in despair was interrupted by a timid knocking at his door. Probably the maid, he thought, coming to clean the fireplace and set the fire for his evening's meal, and so he simply ignored the sound. Sure enough, after a few seconds, there was the scraping sound of a key in the lock and the door creaked open. David heard the maid's quiet footfalls, padding into the room.

"Just clean the grate and set the table for my meal," he said, without opening his eyes, *"You may clean properly tomorrow. I don't want to be disturbed this afternoon."*

There was a short pause, followed by a whispered, *"Yes sir,"* and then there was the sound of the brush in the grate. David sank once more into his unhappy reverie. A moment later the crash of the iron poker on the stone of the fireplace caused him to sit bolt upright and his eyes flew open with a muttered curse.

And there, kneeling at the grate, a beam of late afternoon sunshine turning the tendrils of hair peeking out from beneath her white cotton cap into spun gold, was a vision of such unearthly loveliness that David's heart skipped a beat and his breath caught in his throat.

"Who... who are... who are you?" he stuttered, his eyes feasting upon the pale pink blush suffusing her plump,

youthful cheeks and the hint of tears glistening in her china blue eyes.

"*I'm... I'm so sorry sir,*" she whispered, jumping up and giving David his first glimpse of her perfectly formed figure, which even her long black dress, starched white pinafore and thick black stockings could no nothing to conceal. My God! She was perfection itself!

"*I'm Hannah, sir, Hannah Swan. Molly was ill today and so Mrs Briggs asked me to stand in for her with the gentleman. I'm so sorry sir; I didn't mean to drop the poker. Please... don't tell Mrs Briggs, sir.*"

David had no intention of reporting this lovely creature to the harridan who was his landlady. Transfixed by the fine blue tracery of veins beneath the delicate, milk-white skin at her temples, he felt as if fortune had finally smiled upon him. The clouds of misfortune parted and a brilliant beam of hope shone down from the heavens, accompanied by dancing choirs of angels. Suddenly, completely unexpectedly, here was the answer to all his prayers, right before him. David felt infused with purpose and energy. Inspiration had arrived! He would paint this glorious creature and she would be his muse. And the whole world would marvel at the beauty and perfection of his art.

"*Hannah, come here and sit down. Don't worry about the poker or about the fire. It is destiny that has brought you to my rooms today and we must heed her call!*" David jumped up, grabbed Hannah's arm and led the bemused girl to his armchair, gently pressing on her shoulder to indicate that she should sit down. He then sat down himself in an upright wooden chair as he proceeded to stare intently at the girl's delicate bone structure and watch with captivated fascination the fluttering of her long, dark eyelashes on her pink cheeks.

"Sir... sir I'm sure I don't know what the gentleman means by all of this. I need to get back to my work or Mrs Briggs will be very angry with me," Hannah said, flustered, as her attempt to stand up from the chair was thwarted by David's restraining hand upon her arm.

Although only sixteen, Hannah had seen enough of the world in general, and men in specific, since she had first started work as a maid at thirteen, to know that she needed to be extremely wary of their intentions.

"Hannah, stop worrying. You'll never have to work as a maid again. You are going to be my muse. I'm going to immortalise you in my paintings. You are my salvation and the answer to all my prayers!"

Hannah, who hated being a maid and had always believed that she was intended for better things, narrowed her eyes and looked sideways at David. If she played her cards right, this might just be the answer to her prayers as well! She knew that she needed to secure the best possible deal she could for herself, right now, whilst David's eyes still gleamed with infatuation.

"But, how will that work? How will I take care of myself if I'm spending my time being painted by you, sir," she asked in a breathless voice, allowing her long eyelashes to flutter most becomingly, in a way that she knew was simply irresistible to men. Hannah, despite her youth and seeming innocence, was a smart, ambitious girl and she had observed enough about the way the world worked to broker the best possible deal for herself.

"Hannah, I'll take care of you. Financially, I mean. I'll pay you to be my model; twice as much as you're earning right now! And you won't have to ruin your hands and back or waste your youth doing menial labour. Hannah, my darling,

beauty such as yours should be adored... nay, worshipped. I'm going to make sure that that happens!"

Well, such words were music to the ears of a girl with no prospects other than those of either being a drudge for life, or a quick slap and tickle on the backstairs that might lead to a life of drudgery of an altogether worse kind. Hannah was not the kind of girl to allow such a golden opportunity to escape her grasp.

And so it came to pass that Hannah Swan became David Sinclair's model, muse and, in short order, bed partner. David threw himself, heart and soul, into his dual passions of both loving Hannah, and capturing her essence in his art, and his creativity knew no bounds. He worked obsessively for hours at a stretch, until Hannah, quivering with exhaustion from holding a pose for so long, would burst into tears. David, overcome with remorse, would then gather her up in his arms and shower her with attention and love, food and wine.

He painted Hannah as Diana on the hunt; as Aphrodite with a rose in one hand and a dove in the other; as the Egyptian goddess, Isis, holding aloft an ankh; as a fierce Kali, brandishing the severed heads of her enemies; and as an elaborately helmeted Athena, bearing a shield and spear. He painted her clothed in heavy, ornate costumes from bygone eras; draped in bolts of silks and velvet; swathed in bed sheets; and, very often, dressed in nothing more than the ornate amethyst pendant that had belonged to his grandmother.

He spent hours obsessively mixing paints in an attempt to recreate the exact hue and brilliance of her blue eyes. He would stare at her face with an intensity that felt to Hannah as if it might flay the very skin from her bones. Sitting, standing, reclining, holding flowers, urns, fruit, puppies and, in one rather memorable painting, a black swan (thankfully, for

Hannah's sake, the swan was later added to the painting); Hannah consumed his waking hours and enchanted his dreams. For David this was everything he had ever wished for. He was in Nirvana. He leapt out of bed before dawn, afire with creativity; he painted like a dervish all day and then, at night whilst Hannah slept, he watched her eyelashes fluttering on her sleep-flushed cheeks and painted her some more.

And it seemed as if nothing could go wrong for David. His life truly seemed to be charmed, thanks to the inspiration provided by his muse. The art dealer loved his new work and bought several paintings at a very good price. He received several new commissions, all of which he completed in record time, so that he could speedily return to painting his favourite subject. Such was David's infatuation with Hannah that, even when she wasn't the subject of a painting, he always found a way to paint her into every work he did. Perhaps it was her small, dimpled hand; passing a cup of tea to a society matron he had been commissioned to paint. Perhaps she was a milkmaid in a pastoral scene. Sometimes, when it was impossible to include a depiction of the person of his muse into a painting, he would find a way to use the particular blue of her eyes or the gold of her hair to enliven a boring study of a favourite pet or an adored child. Within months David had paid off all his debts and had sufficient regular income to appoint a new manservant.

David's parents were overjoyed to witness his new dedication to his calling, although David did not enlighten them as to the reason for his success. He knew his mother well enough to be fully aware that she would never approve of his relationship with a servant and would indeed do all in her power to end it. And his father's snobbery and social pretensions would not allow him to countenance a relationship with the serving classes. If either of them recognised in David's paintings his maidservant's features, they made no mention of it. There was a tacit understanding that certain allowances were to be made in support of their son's talent, as long as he kept his indiscretions tactfully well hidden.

And so, Hannah officially stayed in her small attic room in the boarding house, although it was now furnished with several luxuries. But, in reality, she spent most nights ensconced in David's comfortable rooms. Mrs Briggs's discretion was guaranteed through the kind offices of a regular, generous bribe.

When David met his parents' deadline to be financially independent by the end of December, his mother was so pleased that she purchased a smart new town house for him and had it furnished in the latest style. Hannah was given the use of several luxuriously appointed rooms (although officially she was appointed as a maidservant, and slept in the servants' quarters). And so, for several months, both David and Hannah were blissfully happy.

But, inevitably, after almost a year, the initial excitement of not having to wake at dawn to draw water for the boarding house having worn off, Hannah found herself increasingly dissatisfied with her lot in life. Yes, David adored her and showered her with gifts; yes, she ate and drank better than ever before in her life; yes, she was the envy of all the servants and yes, there was a growing stack of paintings celebrating her beauty, which definitely appealed to her vanity. But the life of a model and muse was not all it had promised to be. David required long hours of posing, often dressed in the scantiest of garments, without regard for the weather. And when he was painting he was terribly distracted and hardly heard a word she said. It was boring and tedious and very often cold and uncomfortable. Hannah found herself to be increasingly lonely, as the other servants didn't speak directly to her, but muttered barely audible comments about her moral fibre when she passed them on the stairs. She wasn't able to go out much, as David required her to hang around, waiting for him to require her services.

But by far the biggest problem of all for Hannah was that David refused to introduce her, or to even acknowledge their relationship, to his family. Hannah had, quite early on, realised that David's family was very wealthy, despite the modest apartment in which he had been living when they had first met. She wanted to be a part of that family and her secret desire was for David to legitimize their relationship by marrying her. However, that was never going to happen if she wasn't even formally introduced to his family!

David gave as his excuse that he had no time at present to spend with his family and that he didn't want their special relationship to be tainted by bourgeoisie ideas of fidelity and marriage. But Hannah knew that it was because he was ashamed of her. She had believed him when he had told her that she was the great love of his life, but now she suspected that she was merely his plaything. And, as such, there was every possibility that he would tire of her and eventually cast her out. Already he was no longer as passionate about making love to Hannah every single night and he had gradually begun to find an interest in other subjects to paint.

Hannah knew that she wouldn't get a reference from Mrs Briggs and that, without one, it would be extremely difficult to find another position. And, in any case, she had grown accustomed to a life of comfort and luxury and couldn't imagine working as a maid ever again.

Hannah cursed herself as she realised that she had in fact played her cards very poorly indeed. She should have held out for something more when she still held the upper hand of David's unrequited desire for her. Hannah had hoped that she might force David's hand by becoming pregnant with his child, but alas, the months wore on without any sign of an impending happy event.

Hannah was increasingly ready for a change. She knew that she had to leverage her beauty to find a more congenial situation whilst she still could. Even at the tender age of seventeen, she knew full well that the bloom did not remain forever on the grape.

One day David was out purchasing new art supplies. Hannah was languishing on the chaise lounge, moodily staring out of the window and fervently wishing for something interesting to happen, when the maid arrived to tell her that one of David's loyal patrons, Lord Alfonso Peyton, had arrived to discuss a new commission.

Normally Hannah would have told the maid to inform the patron to return at a later date, but suddenly a new thought gently nudged the edges of her mind. A startling new possibility that she hadn't considered before presented itself and Hannah's heart began pounding against her ribcage in excitement.

Hannah had met Lord Peyton on a previous occasion when he had visited to pick up a painting of his rather rotund, bovine-faced wife and her obscenely fat pug dog. At the time, Hannah had been very aware of the intensity of his focus upon her face and person. She had been introduced as David's model and muse and had been struck by the flicker of interest in the kindly old man's eyes. She had turned away from his scrutiny, immediately dismissing his obvious interest from her mind. What use had she at the time for the attentions of the large, grizzled old man with a potato nose when she was the darling of a gorgeous, successful young artist? But now, a year later, she saw things in a different light. If David really was losing interest in her, then the only sensible thing to do was to secure her future. And what better way to do that than to gain the patronage of a wealthy and titled old man, who would treat her with adoration and give her the attention that she deserved, Hannah reasoned.

When the maidservant showed Lord Peyton into the drawing room, the instant spark of desire which Hannah could quite clearly see lighting up his eyes, proved that she had not been wrong to consider the possibilities that this prospect offered her. If the old man was surprised to find Hannah unaccompanied, his good breeding did not allow him to show it, and he took the situation in his stride. Indeed, he was rather pleased to have the delightful young lady to himself for a couple of hours.

Hannah was at her most charming and witty that afternoon, subtly flattering the old man and taking care to position herself so that the afternoon sunlight lit up her hair in a golden halo around her face and highlighted the soft smoothness of her pink cheeks. One lesson Hannah had mastered over the past year as a painter's model was to display herself to her very best advantage.

After tea, just as Lord Peyton was starting to think of taking his leave, as David had not yet made his appearance, Hannah decided that the time had come to play her hand. Checking to see that she had the old man's full attention, Hannah softly sighed and allowed tears to glisten in her huge blue eyes, before turning to stare out of the window in quarter profile, ensuring that her best side was on display. After a full count of three, she permitted a small sob to escape her lips, before capturing her plump lower lip between her teeth and allowing her eyelashes to flutter most becomingly upon her rosy cheeks. In the presence of such a consummate professional, Lord Peyton simply didn't stand a chance and he gobbled up the bait, hook, line and sinker.

After several heartfelt entreaties from the kindly old man to divulge what ailed her, Hannah lowered her voice to a whisper and spun an incredible tale of cruelty and neglect. Hannah had to dial the pathos back a little when Lord Peyton leapt to his feet with the resolve to, "*Call that scoundrel out to a duel!*" However, without much difficulty, she was able to convince her would-be rescuer that the best course of action would be to forthwith remove her from her demeaning life of servitude and set her up in a small apartment of her own, where, Hannah intimated with demurely lowered lashes, she would suitably express her gratitude to her chivalrous rescuer.

And so it was that, when David finally returned home that evening, he found Hannah gone; all the clothing and jewellery he had given her missing from her wardrobe and the servants unable to supply him with any clues as to her whereabouts. If it had not been for the brief note that Hannah had left on the mantelpiece that read, "*David, I've left you and I'm not coming back. Sorry. H,*" David would have been inclined to believe that she had been kidnapped. He was absolutely beside himself with grief. He simply couldn't believe that his beautiful muse had abandoned him. He berated himself, over and over again, for his shoddy treatment and his woeful neglect of her and promised himself that he would make it up to her as soon as she was safely home again. Alas, this was not to be.

David spent every penny he had trying to locate Hannah, but, with the considerable resources of Lord Peyton at her disposal, she had covered her tracks well. Over the next few weeks David steadily fell apart. He stopped painting; spending every hour of every day staring at his beloved, immortalised in oils. He felt as if a part of his soul had been ripped out and he began drinking heavily again to anaesthetise the pain. Soon he was frequenting opium dens several times a week in an attempt to escape, for a few, brief hours, his sorry plight.

Matters worsened so much that David's mother even put her principles aside and engaged the services of a private detective to find Hannah. Eventually these efforts paid off and Hannah was found to be living in a luxurious bijoux apartment in a small coastal town, as the mistress of Lord Peyton. When a letter begging Hannah to return to David did not elicit the desired response, Catherine put her pride in her pocket and went to visit her son's beloved ex-muse. She had reached the rather startling realisation that her son's health and well-being were worth far more to her than her social standing.

Catherine offered Hannah a considerable sum of money to work once more as David's model and muse. However Hannah point-blank refused. She had great hopes of Lord Peyton asking for her hand in marriage, once the official mourning period for his wife, who had subsequently died, was over. The life of a muse and model simply couldn't compare to the possibility of becoming a Lady, who stood to inherit a vast fortune upon her husband's death. An event which Hannah believed would take place in the not too distant future, as Lord Peyton was more than four times her age.

Catherine did not divulge to her son that she had discovered Hannah's whereabouts, nor did she tell him of her subsequent visit to Hannah. Instead she tried all manner of other diversions to lift him out of his funk. She generously offered a Grande Tour of Europe, which he declined with a mere shrug of his shoulders. She suggested a seaside holiday, to which suggestion he didn't even deign to respond, merely drawing his grubby robe closer to his emaciated chest and closing his eyes to signal that the conversation was over. James Sinclair tried reasoning with his son, which yielded absolutely no results whatsoever, and several of David's erstwhile friends were roped in by Catherine to try and get through to her grieving son.

Catherine even took the drastic step of appointing a lovely young housemaid, who bore a passing resemblance to Hannah, in an attempt to entice David into taking up with another muse. But David didn't even notice the girl, so caught up was he in his own misery. All he did was drown his sorrows every night and then sleep off the effects of the alcohol until past noon the following day.

Two months after Hannah had left him, David was discovered by the selfsame lovely young maid, lying on the floor of his luxuriously-appointed townhouse with a bullet through his brain.

"Wow, that was an unexpectedly abrupt ending to the story! What a wasted life. All that talent and ability; all those opportunities and privilege, all for naught," I remarked.

"Indeed this life was cut short at a relatively young age. But it certainly wasn't a wasted life," replied the Green Lady. *"There was much to be learned. As we have already*

discussed, the lifetime as Jean-Philippe was all about ego in the driver's seat.

However, in the early life of David Sinclair, ego took a backseat. In fact, David struggled to find the energy or enthusiasm to do anything much at all. His ego was pretty much waiting for direction, which is the way it should be. The ego should always be directed by the heart. Unfortunately, in David's case, it wasn't his higher self, via the heart portal, that finally set him on his life's course, but rather his infatuation with another being. Infatuation, which quickly became obsession. Instead of finding his direction from within himself, he externalised his heart connection in the form of Hannah. She became his raison d'être; his entire world. Instead of finding his own truth within himself, he found it in his fascination with the beauty of Hannah. And we see the consequences of that decision in the way in which his life spiralled out of control when the centre was removed from his life."

"Hannah was certainly a calculating little miss. I really don't know how David didn't see that!" I scoffed.

"Well, he saw exactly what he wanted to see. He wasn't actually interested in whom Hannah truly was, but rather in the two-dimensional beauty that he had created her to be in his mind. The relationship was doomed to fail. But obviously this contract was set up pre-incarnationally, and each learned from the interaction what they most needed to teach themselves. And that includes David's parents, Lord Peyton and many other role players as well."

"I have a question, though; something that has always bothered me. What happens when a person commits suicide? Are they truly doomed for all eternity, as many religions would have us believe? And did David have a choice?

What would have happened if he had not committed suicide, but had gone on to live a long, full life?" I asked.

The Green Lady responded, "*Well firstly, of course David had free will, which he exercised in killing himself. Had he not done so, then he would have had the opportunity to learn many additional lessons during his lifetime. But, choosing to end a lifetime in suicide definitely doesn't lead to eternal damnation. Such beings are, however, generally extremely traumatised once they are back in the spirit world and often require much healing and counselling by their guides and other higher beings before they are able to reincarnate again. There is certainly no punishment for suicide, other than the extreme, self-inflicted emotional and psycho-spiritual trauma of the personality that leads up to the taking of such a drastic step.*

In David's case, his guide, Michael, had to work with him for quite some time in order to gently heal him and bring him back to the point of being willing to experience another lifetime. At the end of this time, however, David still held the firm belief that his considerable gifts and talents had led to him being emotionally unstable and susceptible to extreme acts. This was one of the reasons why David elected to reincarnate as someone with limited capacity in his next lifetime. He also wanted to ensure that he would have to find his own heart portal to his inner divinity and not again make the mistake of placing his ok-ness in another. So, his next lifetime would not have access to exceptional talents, abilities, charm, intellect or good looks."

"*Wow, it sounds like he decided to choose to considerably limit his next lifetime! I'm very interested in hearing all about how that decision worked out for him.*"

"Very well, then. We'll continue with the story of the next lifetime when we meet again, next week..."

CHAPTER 6:
HEART IN THE DRIVER'S SEAT

"Peter, the next lifetime chosen was that of a boy called Rodney, or Oddie, as he was known by many at the time. This is a story of a very different set of choices to the lifetimes as Jean-Philippe and David Sinclair. Instead of ego, the heart was allowed to be in control and the personality itself had none of the talents, abilities and privilege that both the prior lifetimes had enjoyed. In fact, most would have deemed the next life to have been one of diminished capacity and, subsequently, rather small and limited. But, decide for yourself..."

The small boy huddled in the pitch dark, at the bottom of the disused mineshaft, covering his eyes with his hands and shivering with fear and cold. *"Please Jesus, don't let them find me. Please Jesus, make them go away!"* he prayed, his lips silently mouthing the words. *"Please Jesus... Oh no!"* he gasped with terror as he heard a loud shout, really close to the opening of the mineshaft, followed by a mocking falsetto, *"Ooooo-ooddie, oh Ooooddie... where are yooou? Come out, come out, come out and plaaayy!"* Rodney cowered even closer to the rough earth wall, whimpering and quivering as a hot stream of urine ran uncontrolled down his leg.

"*Come, Oddie, Oddie, Oddie, come on out. We just wanna play with you!*" It was David Johnston, his most determined tormentor, and Rodney shuddered as he remembered what David and his cronies had done to him the last time they had caught him alone after school.

Rodney had been given his hateful nickname on the very first day of school by his nemesis, David Johnston, or Johnnie, as he was known. The teacher had asked Rodney to stand up and introduce himself to the class and he had reluctantly risen to his feet, only to stand for a full minute before he could finally force the words out. "*I... I... I'm...I'm Ro... Ro... Ro... odd...y,*" he stammered, sitting back down again with burning ears and a pounding heart, trying not to notice the delighted grins of his classmates. And that was all it took. During the first break he was surrounded by a group of six boys, all chanting, "*Odd-die, Odd-die, Odd-die!*" and grabbing at his hair and his clothing. "*Puh... puh... puhlease... don... don... don't do tha... tha... that!*" Rodney stammered, which only caused his tormentors to redouble their efforts. By the time break was over, he looked as if he'd been dragged through a bramble bush backwards: his hair awry, his shirt hanging out of his trousers and his face covered in tears and snot.

That first day of school was only the beginning of Rodney's ongoing torment. As the boys grew older, their mockery of Rodney became more and more physically violent, until Rodney returned home most days covered in scratches and bruises, his school books torn and his clothing filthy or missing entirely. The invisible emotional damage was far worse, of course. Rodney's mother reported the bullying to the headmaster time-and-time again and Johnnie and his cronies were punished over-and-over again. It didn't stop the bullying. It simply made the bullies more inventive and more vicious. Rodney was just too easy a target and just too much fun to torment.

Rodney's mother, Edith, had been thirty-four when she had given birth to Rodney. She had always been a quiet, shy, plain girl and had accepted early on that she would probably never find a husband or have children of her own. What man could possibly be interested in her? She resigned herself to living at home and taking care of her parents as they grew older. This was a perfectly respectable life choice for a single woman at the time.

During the war, Edith joined the Red Cross to do her bit for the war effort. It was during her shift at the local hospital that she met Evan Adams. Evan had been badly injured and had been sent back home from the front to recover. When Edith first saw him lying unconscious in bed, his pale face of scarcely darker hue than the bandage around his head, she thought she had never beheld a more handsome man in all her life. And, as Evan slowly regained his health, Edith fell deeper and deeper in love with the charming, happy-go-lucky, flirtatious soldier. Evan, who was only twenty-five at the time, wasn't really interested in Edith, but he enjoyed making her blush, and flirting with her provided some welcome distraction from the boredom of being bed-ridden.

Eventually Evan's wounds healed sufficiently for him to be sent back to the front, but before he departed, he left Edith with a gift and a burden that would define the rest of her days. On Evan's final night before being re-deployed, he invited Edith out for a drink, ostensibly to say thank you for her devoted care. The drink turned into much more and Edith lost her virginity that night to the man of her dreams. She believed him when he said that he loved her and, for years afterwards, she still believed that Evan would come back from the war, marry her and provide her illegitimate son with a much-needed father.

What Edith didn't know was that she was not the only woman bedded by Evan that night - she was merely the most convenient first. And, although he promised to write, Evan had never had any intention of doing so. After all, dear old Edith wasn't exactly his idea of the perfect sweetheart and she certainly wasn't marriageable material either. It was laughable - she was far too old, being almost ten years older than Evan, and not nearly pretty enough. Evan was killed in action four months later and died without ever thinking of Edith again.

Edith, on the other hand, thought of Evan every single day of her life for the next twenty years until she died of breast cancer, still living in the small cottage that she had inherited from her parents, for whom she had cared until the end of their days. Despite the stigma of being an unmarried mother, Edith's parents had supported her and allowed her to continue living at home, for which she had always been extremely grateful. She never learned of Evan's death so soon after their parting and she was to live in hope of his returning for the rest of her life. Rodney, in turn, inherited the cottage from Edith and he too was to remain living there until his own death.

Edith adored her son and provided him with the best loving care and attention that she could. She looked forward to the day that Evan would return from the war and they could set up home together. In anticipation of this joyful event,

Edith began referring to herself as Mrs Adams and she took to wearing her mother's gold wedding band which had become too tight for her mother to wear. In time most of her friends and neighbours forgot that Edith wasn't really married and they too began referring to her as Mrs Adams.

Rodney, despite his mother's loving care and focussed attention, and in stark contrast to the sparkling intellect and charm of his father, had always been slow. He was slow to walk, slow to talk and he struggled to learn how to do the most basic things, such as tying his shoelaces, buttoning up his clothing or catching a ball. Edith's family doctor could find nothing physically wrong with the boy and so, when Rodney was six, he referred Edith to a child development specialist, Dr. Stanley Morrison. Dr Morrison conducted numerous tests on the boy, including an IQ test.

As Dr Morrison explained to Edith during an interview in his offices a week later, "*Mrs Adams, Rodney's IQ tested at 75. Although this is lower than the average IQ of 85-115, it is not low enough to qualify Rodney for the special education which is provided for children with a disability. The other tests that I have conducted also indicate that Rodney isn't mentally disabled; he is merely a slow learner. I am recommending that Rodney be placed in a normal school, where he should be able to acquire a basic education, which will equip him for a useful life.*

Rodney will, however, require extra support at home and after school hours. I would suggest extra repetition of lessons and additional tutoring. It might also be a good idea to encourage other activities and interests that could provide a living when his schooling is complete. Mrs Adams, please don't be discouraged. Rodney has every chance at living a good and useful life."

And so Rodney was duly enrolled in the local primary school at the age of six, which was when his troubles really began.

Eventually Johnnie and the other boys tired of searching for Rodney in the disused mine shafts and returned to the field behind the school yard to kick around an old tin can. Rodney finally emerged from the mine shaft just before dark and made his weary way home.

Edith made no comment when she opened the door to find her son on the doorstep, a big wet patch on the front of his serge shorts, and his Fair Isle pull-over covered in mud, but merely marched him upstairs to the bathroom and made a silent vow to herself to address the bullies once-and-for-all.

That evening, she cuddled the freshly-bathed and warmly-wrapped boy on her lap and whispered into his ear, "*I love you, my boy. You are important and special and don't ever let anyone tell you anything else! You are going to live a wonderful life and make many people happy, just as you've made me happy, every single day of your life, since the very first day I held you in my arms as a tiny baby.*"

"*Bu... but... the oth... other b... bo... boys ha... hate me!*" Rodney wailed.

"*They don't hate you, my boy. They hate themselves. They're afraid that someone will find out just how much they hate themselves and so they have to take out that hate on someone else. You mustn't hate them for what they do. Rather feel compassion for them.*"

Edith tried to encourage Rodney to develop outside interests, just as the expert had advised. But most of these attempts ended in disaster. Rodney lacked the co-ordination to be any good at ball games and most of his forays into athletic endeavours resulted in further mockery by his peers, as he struggled in last in track events or dropped the shot-put on his foot or nearly drowned several times whilst trying to learn to swim.

Although Rodney struggled to feel compassion for his tormentors, when he was twelve, Johnnie's father, who was a coal miner, was involved in an accident and was carried out of the mine shaft with both legs crushed. Two agonising days later he succumbed to his injuries. Johnnie was removed from school for the funeral and he never returned, as his mother took the children to live with their grandparents.

With their ringleader gone and puberty beckoning, the other boys turned to alternative pursuits and the worst days of Rodney's torment were in the past. However, he remained a loner, preferring to stay indoors in the library during break, either doing his homework or paging through books about birds. Because, finally, Rodney had developed an outside interest after all.

It had happened whilst he was hiding away from the school bullies in a small copse some distance from the abandoned mineshafts. Rodney had discovered the perfect hiding place. It was a natural alcove created by a massive old tree trunk, half buried in the ground. Anyone passing within even a few feet of the hiding place would not have been aware of its existence and Rodney was to spend many hours there, hiding away and day dreaming.

One late afternoon in spring Rodney suddenly became aware of the cacophony of birdsong in the copse. Later on he couldn't explain why he had never been aware of it before that day. Perhaps he had simply been too caught up in his own miseries. But on that particular day, the birdsong suddenly sounded to him like the most beautiful sound he had ever heard.

Peeping out from behind the tree trunk, he noticed a tiny brown wren warbling away on a branch and he was struck by how very perfect and beautiful it was. He forgot all about his troubles as he sat for another two hours just watching the birds and listening to their song, which earned him a scolding from his mother when he returned home very late for his tea. But Rodney didn't care - he had finally found his passion.

After that day he spent every spare moment either bird watching, or trying to identify in a bird atlas, the birds he had seen on his walks. He learnt to identify any bird by their call and also to imitate the bird calls. In time, he was able to call the birds to himself and he spent blissful hours surrounded by birds of all kinds, studying them at close range. Edith was thrilled with Rodney's new hobby and she encouraged him by supplying him with every bird book she could possibly afford. Rodney's walks took him far afield and he grew strong and fit in the pursuit of his passion.

When Rodney was sixteen he left school. There was no point in staying any longer as he had already been kept back twice and was no longer progressing in his studies. He had, it seemed, reached the limit of his intellectual capacity. He could read and write, albeit slowly, and do basic arithmetic, which would probably, Edith reasoned, be enough for him to get a job that would support him in a simple life.

Edith found Rodney a job with a local carpenter. Rodney was employed at minimum wage to dust and sweep the workshop and to do basic jobs such as packing and deliveries. In time, the carpenter, who was a kind man and a bachelor who had always had a soft spot for Edith, taught Rodney to make small, simple wooden items such as shelves and spice racks and cutting boards. Rodney was given a share of the profits from the sale of these items and this allowed him to purchase more bird books and supplies for his hobby. As Rodney's skills improved, he asked the carpenter to teach him how to make wooden birdhouses and in time these became quite sought after.

Rodney remained a loner who preferred to spend his time on his hobbies of birdwatching and woodworking rather than on social activities. However, there were certain people whose company Rodney always welcomed - children.

It had all happened so unexpectedly. One sunny Saturday morning Rodney was in the copse, right next to the fallen tree trunk where he had hidden so many times before as a young boy. He was engaged in his favourite hobby when he heard children shouting. Suddenly there was a crashing through the trees and a small boy came rushing past Rodney, his chest heaving and his eyes wildly searching for a place to hide.

Without stopping to think, Rodney called out to the boy, "*Hi... hi... hide here!*" and pulled aside the greenery covering the entrance to the hiding place. The small boy looked up at Rodney with terror in his eyes and then darted inside and Rodney pulled the fronds back in place just in time. Two larger boys came crashing into the copse, shouting, "*Frankie, come back here, you little twerp! We'll get you this time for sure!*" and then they came to a halt as they were confronted by an angry Rodney, brandishing a stick. "*Whoa, man! What do you think you're doing?*" the larger of the two boys said, fear starting to enter his voice as Rodney advanced upon him, waving the stick about with a fierce expression on his face. "*Hey, mister, we're not doing anything wrong. Let us go! Please mister, don't hurt us!*" the smaller of the two boys said, with a quiver in his voice. Then, as Rodney shook the stick at them again, they both turned tail and ran, as fast as they could, to get away from the mad man in the woods.

After waiting for a while to ensure that they would not return, Rodney pulled aside the greenery hiding the small boy, who climbed out, saying, "*Thanks, mister. Dunno what I would have done if you'd not been here today. Those bullies are always coming after me. I hate 'em!*" Rodney threw down his stick and beckoned to the boy, showing him a nest with four perfect eggs in it, hidden away inside a bush. This was the beginning of a beautiful friendship.

Frankie started spending all his free time with Rodney, who taught Frankie all he knew about birds. It was the first real friend Rodney had ever had. In time, Frankie brought other friends to meet Rodney and so Rodney became known amongst the local children as the Birdman. He was always kind and patient and willing to share his knowledge.

And so the years passed. In time, the carpenter passed away but Rodney was able to support his very modest lifestyle through the sale of his wooden bird houses. He was content with his life.

One morning, shortly after his fifty-fourth birthday, Rodney was standing on a ladder in his garden, checking a nest to see whether the eggs inside had hatched. He overbalanced and fell. His neighbour discovered him later that morning when she arrived at his front door with a batch of freshly-baked scones and, alarmed by the lack of response to her knocking, decided to investigate. The doctors said that Rodney had suffered a massive coronary attack, which was why he had fallen off the ladder in the first place, and, during the autopsy, it was discovered that he had died due to a defective heart.

At Rodney's funeral the church was packed with small children and all those congregated agreed that they had never seen so many birds in the graveyard at that time of the year.

"*Well, that was a rather sad little tale. What an ordinary and rather unsuccessful life poor old Oddie had! He started out at a serious disadvantage and he never really amounted to anything much!*" I remarked, feeling rather let down as I packed my notebook away.

"*Oh, Peter, have you learnt nothing during these sessions of ours?*" the Green Lady sighed in exasperation. "*Rodney's life was a remarkably successful one. Don't you see that the achievements and accolades and wealth that the ego-mind deems important are less than nothing to the soul? Those things are simply illusions of this world and they don't last beyond the death of the personality. The things of true, lasting importance are the gifts of the soul.*

Rodney's diminished intellectual capacity caused him to develop his heart connection. He found something that he loved and he found a way to share that love with others. In so doing, he lived a beautiful and meaningful life. He found true happiness and, more importantly and far more unusually, real contentment. He discovered his true, lasting value and didn't make the mistake of believing that his value was to be found in his achievements or his possessions or his wealth. A successful life indeed."

"*Well... I don't really know what to make of that!*" I said, feeling rather confused. "*It seems to me that all the things that we believe add up to a successful life, are not worth a whole lot after all!*"

"Peter, the measure of a successful life is the degree to which you have been able to find, and express, your most authentic self in that lifetime. The degree to which you have been able to find your own truth, regardless of what the world outside of you tells you is important and real and true. The degree to which you have been able to follow the promptings of your heart, instead of being driven by the fears of your ego.

Remember, these lives are merely stories that we are telling ourselves. What is real and true are the spiritual gifts that we discover and express during our lives."

"Well, then, I can't wait to hear what next week's story will bring," I said.

"Next week we will explore a lifetime of integration of many of the experiences and lessons from the previous lives we have encountered. This will be the lifetime of finding the connecting threads and of weaving the stories together so that they begin to make sense."

"That sounds like an interesting story. OK then, I'll see you next week," I called after the Green Lady as she disappeared between the trees.

Chapter 7:
Weaving Together the
Threads (part 1)

" *P*eter, today's story is set in a time and place that will feel familiar to you, namely, the twenty-first century city of Johannesburg in South Africa. This story describes what is generally known as an ascension lifetime."

"I've heard that term used before. In fact, you mentioned it during the story of Deena. I recall that the Lemurians ascended their civilisation as a whole. But I'm unsure of exactly what that means."

"As I've mentioned to you before, there is no time outside of this reality that you currently inhabit, and so all lifetimes actually happen at the same time. However, there is some form of sequentiality, meaning that certain events only happen once other events have already happened.

In addition, all events and all perspectives are eternally valid, which means that each moment will continue to exist in eternity. Each lifetime is made up of a series of moments, all of which will always exist - nothing is ever lost. All events are also linked. Since the human mind is a product of time-bound sequentiality, these concepts will be quite difficult for you to understand. But I will explain it all to you *using the metaphor of Indra's net, which we encountered before.*

Each life reflects all the other lives and each life is affected by all the other lives too. This means that a change made in one life will change the other lives as well. It is never 'too late' and a lifetime is never actually over. The individual moments that make up a lifetime are, as I have already said, eternally valid - they will always exist and it's possible to visit any of these moments and make changes that will profoundly affect all other lives, just as in Indra's web."

"Well, just like before, I find that thought mind-boggling! Why have you told me all of this? What does this have to do with this so-called ascension lifetime?"

"Because you will require this understanding in order to benefit from the next story I am about to tell you! The reason we call the lifetime of Elizabeth, whose story this is, an ascension lifetime, is that Elizabeth is the part of self who engages in the journey of seeking such deep healing of her own psyche, that she finds herself addressing the outstanding issues from all of her other lifetimes too.

In so doing, she raises the frequency of her consciousness and ascends her unified soul out of that level of this reality. If any parts of self are lost, stuck or left behind, an incomplete ascension occurs and the self remains attached to this reality. All parts of self need to be healed and brought back to unity for the self to be released, to either continue its journey through other realities or to sublimate back into the Oneness. So a perfect ascension is always the final, great work of the soul."

"But, how will you know if it is your so-called ascension lifetime?"

"Because you will choose for it to be so! You will be done with playing the game of duality and you will be aching to return to unity-consciousness. The shiny illusions of your current reality will no longer appeal to you and you will be seeking the true gifts of the soul, rather than the temporary enticements of this world. The metaphor of Indra's web is useful here too, as the fact that all jewels are simply a reflection of all other jewels implies the illusory nature of all appearances. Appearances are therefore not reality, but merely a reflection of reality.

But why don't I tell you the story and you can see if it doesn't become clearer to you once I have finished doing so?"

"I'm all ears and very eager to hear this story."

"Good, then let us begin..."

"Elizabeth, as your psychologist, I really feel that I have helped you as far as I am able to, at this point in time. The anti-depressants prescribed by your psychiatrist and the cognitive behavioural therapy we have applied during the past six months have definitely assisted you in learning to control and manage your panic attacks. We have made excellent progress, as evidenced by the fact that you are no longer experiencing any panic attacks.

However, I know that you are convinced that there is a deeper spiritual reason for these attacks, which we have not adequately addressed in our sessions together. I am aware of the fact that you believe that the deep roots of your panic attacks lie in past-lives, but I am simply not trained or equipped to assist you any further with such past-life issues.

I am going to recommend that you work with a very competent and experienced hypnotherapist to guide you toward finding the messages hidden in these vivid memories and dreams of previous lifetimes that you are experiencing. A hypnotherapist will be able to assist you in releasing any karma or other attachments associated with any of your incarnations.

You are well aware that my personal belief system does not actually stretch to a belief in prior incarnations, but I know that your experiences over the past six months have convinced you of their veracity. Therefore, I believe that you need to work with someone who shares your belief system, and can assist you on that level. In addition, the hypnotherapist you use will need to be able to "contain" the experience in a safe space because, as we have already seen, it can get very emotional and quite frightening at times to view these lives.

I'm going to recommend that you see a trusted colleague of mine, Sarah Cavanaugh, who is a trained psychologist and hypnotherapist, as well as being a shaman and a truly gifted spiritual healer. I am convinced that she has the perfect combination of skills and experience to help you get to the bottom of your concerns.

I'm certain that Sarah will be able to assist you in satisfying your curiosity about these so-called past-lives. More importantly, she will also be able to help you to release all blockages or attachments that are negatively impacting upon your current life."

Elizabeth listened carefully to what her psychologist had to say and then responded, "*Of course I am curious about my past lives and would like to explore them further for interest's sake. As you've already said, I have several inexplicable, vivid memories, which are definitely not from this lifetime as Elizabeth, nor from any movie I have seen or any book I have ever read. But, for me, it's probably more about addressing any outstanding issues in any of my lives and releasing blockages or attachments. I need to finally completely resolve the root cause of my panic attacks, not merely manage them so that they no longer impact upon my life and my career. I think that visiting my past-lives will enable me to do so."*

"Elizabeth, I know that you think that your problem is the panic attacks. But, I can assure you, the panic attacks are only a symptom of a far deeper issue which is ready to be addressed. In time you will come to bless these panic attacks as the means by which you will attain a whole new level of awareness. Just be prepared for some life-altering experiences with Sarah Kavanaugh. You may find that you will never be the same again!"

"Well, I'm prepared to take that chance! Perhaps it's time for me to change. I'll contact the hypnotherapist you recommended and see what she can do for me."

Elizabeth Aiken had always been a top achiever. Her mother had been the full-time, live-in domestic worker of Lynn and Barry du Preez, two academics at the University of the Witwatersrand in Johannesburg, South Africa. Lynn, a large, strident, dishevelled activist of a woman, was a Professor of Women's Studies and Barry was a distracted, dumpy and brilliant Professor of Molecular Biology, and a world-renowned expert in the development of veterinary vaccines.

Lynn and Barry were both in their early forties when their domestic worker of five years, Lydia, admitted to Lynn that she was pregnant. Lydia, who had been involved with a succession of abusive men and who was one of Lynn's pet projects, uncharacteristically was unwilling to disclose the identity of the father of her unborn child. Lynn promised Lydia that she would be taken care of during her pregnancy and that the child would receive proper care and an education. In this matter, as with most things, Barry simply withdrew into his study and left his wife to get on with it.

And so Lydia received the best maternal care as she grew heavy with child, and the du Preez house grew ever more untidy, dusty and uncared for. Lynn and Barry hardly noticed. They had far more important academic matters on their minds.

Lydia was duly delivered of a healthy baby girl at an upmarket private clinic, paid for by the du Preez's. This was a necessity as this was during the 1970's and the heyday of apartheid in South Africa. Lydia, as a black woman, would not have been allowed to have her child in one of better, whites-only state hospitals and Lynn was adamant that both Lydia and the baby receive the best possible care.

Lynn was somewhat taken aback when she viewed the baby Elizabeth for the first time. Elizabeth was white! Or, certainly, a very pale, cafe-latte colour. Lynn looked questioningly at Lydia, who stared right back in defiant silence. And so it was. As a committed feminist, Lynn would never have dreamed of forcing Lydia to reveal the identity of the baby's father or of reneging on her promise to raise and school the child.

And so Lydia and Elizabeth returned to the du Preez household, where they were ensconced in style in the guest bedroom. Lynn gave up on expecting any cleaning services from Lydia. Lydia's only job now was to raise her child. Four months later, Lynn reluctantly employed another domestic worker, Siena, who now lived in the servant's quarters whilst

Lydia and Elizabeth lived a life of leisure and were paid for doing so by the du Preez's.

Then, one morning, Lynn awoke to the sound of Elizabeth crying. She waited a while for Lydia to calm the child, but Elizabeth's screams only increased in volume. And so, with a sigh, she put on her slippers and walked down the passage to the guest bedroom, reflecting as she did so that she had chosen not to have children for this very reason and yet, here she was, saddled with the responsibility of another woman's child.

Lynn discovered Elizabeth tightly wrapped in a blanket in her cot, but there was no sign at all of Lydia. Lynn walked through the house calling for Lydia and eventually returned to the guest bedroom, where she discovered a scrawled note written in a childish hand on a piece of blue-lined exercise-book paper on the pedestal.

"Madam. I must go and never come back. I have a new man to take care of me now. Elizabeth she is the child of the boss. Madam must care for her now. Madam promised. Lydia."

Lynn sank to the floor as her legs gave way beneath her. She sat clutching the note in a shaking hand as she gasped and choked, desperately trying to persuade her lungs to function normally again.

After what seemed like an eternity, Lynn pulled herself to her feet and shuffled, like a very old woman, to her bedroom, where she thrust the note into Barry's hand and then turned and walked into the kitchen where she put on the kettle for tea.

"Lynn, please... I'm so sorry... What can I say? It was just... well, it was just... It was nothing really." Barry put a tentative hand on Lynn's shoulder and then stepped back in

shock as she turned around and slapped him hard through the face.

"*You little shit! How can you say it was nothing! You took advantage of a poor, uneducated, black woman who was living under our roof, under our protection. You are the worst possible kind of male chauvinist pig! I can't even bear to look at you!*"

"*Lynn, it wasn't like that, I promise. Lydia... she... she came onto me!*"

"*Oh get away from me! You make me sick!*" Lynn shrieked, collapsing into a chair where she began to moan and weep; deep, wracking sobs at the betrayal and at the destruction of her life and her marriage.

Barry stood a few metres away, his hands raised in supplication, dithering, not knowing what to do. But then Elizabeth's screams became even more urgent and, seeing as Lynn clearly wasn't going to do anything about the baby, he realised that he would have to step up to the plate and manage the situation before the neighbours arrived to investigate. Or worse still, he thought with a gulp, perhaps called the police. He would be arrested if the situation was brought to the attention of the authorities.

The South African Immorality Act of 1950 prohibited sexual intercourse between whites and non-whites and Barry would be charged and possibly sentenced to at least five years in prison. He felt a small, secret sense of relief when he remembered that The Prohibition of Mixed Marriages Act of 1949 ensured that he wouldn't be able to make an honest woman out of Lydia. Besides, she seemed to have abandoned her child to leave with another man. The fear focussed Barry's vague and distracted academic mind and he rushed into the guest bedroom to manage the situation.

Elizabeth was purple in the face and her screams were truly remarkably loud for such a tiny thing. But, when Barry picked her up and held her to his chest, she gradually calmed down. And after he had, very clumsily, changed her nappy and heated up and fed to Elizabeth one of the bottles of milk that he found in the fridge, peace and quiet finally returned to the du Preez household.

Barry looked down at the red, tear-stained face and the little hand grasping his finger as the infant furiously sucked at the teat and he felt something very strange happen inside of him. A massive, warm wave of love broke inside his chest and then rose up again to well over into tears. For the first time in his quiet, introverted life, Barry du Preez felt true love and connection to another human being. Of course he was fond of Lynn and certain members of his family, but this fierce, protective love; this overwhelming sense of helpless wonder at the miracle he held in his arms; this was completely unprecedented and totally unexpected. And right there, in the guest bedroom, Barry du Preez fell in love. And he knew that he would do anything in the world to prevent this child from being hurt or from being taken away from him.

Lynn, who wasn't in general given to histrionics and who mostly adopted a pragmatic approach to life, had in the meantime mopped up her tears with the dishcloth and taken stock of the situation. Although she was still furious with Barry, a tiny voice inside her head told her that she had, on some level, known what was going on between Lydia and Barry and had chosen to ignore that fact. The very first time Lynn had interviewed Lydia for the position, she had had serious misgivings. There had been something so very sensual about the way Lydia had swung her hips as she walked into the living room, her ample bosom straining against the buttons of her modest dress. And though she had kept her eyes demurely downcast for the interview, there had been a touch of insolence in her responses. Lynn had chosen to ignore all of this because she had been so desperate to find a domestic worker and also because she was always so determined to help all victims of patriarchy, wherever she encountered them.

Over the years, Lydia's insolence towards Lynn had increased, and the house was barely kept clean. However, Lynn had noticed that Lydia was very friendly toward Barry and that she swayed her hips even more when he was around and fluttered her eyelashes when she served him his tea. Lynn had turned a blind eye to all of this, reminding herself that Lydia had not had any advantages, due to her race, and also that she, Lynn, was duty-bound to care for her less advantaged sisters. Also, it was simply too much effort to try and address Lydia's attitude, as Lynn was a very busy academic, caught up in a hectic teaching schedule and the need to publish in order to maintain her funding.

Lynn and Barry's marriage had long ago become one of convenience only. In fact, it had probably even started out that way. They had agreed from the very beginning that children would be out of the question. Lynn was a career woman and there were so many unwanted children in the world that she couldn't, in all conscience, add to the number. But the marriage suited both of them. It was convenient to have a life partner and they rubbed along well. Lynn was very happy with their life together and didn't want to go through the misery of a divorce and the humiliating effort of dividing up their belongings. It would simply be easier to stay married. In time they would get past this difficulty and life would go on as usual.

Lynn had just decided all of this when Barry walked into the kitchen, carrying the baby in his arms; an unaccustomed expression of determination in his eyes.

"Lynn, I'm really sorry about all of this. I know what I've done is unforgivable, and you have every right to be furious with me. But, as you know, you and I haven't had a physical relationship for years and I guess it was just a moment of weakness. It only happened the once and I immediately regretted it afterwards. It was when you were away at the conference last December. I suppose I was feeling lonely. I had had a bad day at work and I came home and drank a couple of glasses of whisky. I never intended for it to happen, but Lydia was there and she was sweet and comforting and...

Well, I told Lydia that it could never happen again. It never actually occurred to me that the baby could be mine. But, now that I know that it is... Lynn, I'm keeping her. She's my responsibility and I want to do the right thing. I'll understand if you want to leave me, but I really hope that you don't. We have a very good life together. You know as well as I do what Lydia is like. She's not going to be willing or able to take care of this child and I can't bear the thought of little Elizabeth being hurt or deprived of anything she needs." Barry's voice broke on this last sentence and Lynn was astonished to see the resolve and love shining through the tears in his eyes. She had never seen Barry this way before. Suddenly he was focussed and determined. Suddenly he was acting like a man and not like a vague academic and, for the first time ever, Lynn felt a small spark of admiration and respect for her husband as a man.

It took some time and concerted effort, but in the end Barry did convince Lynn to keep Elizabeth. She felt it was their duty to do so and she had never seen Barry so happy before. Granting Barry his wish with respect to Elizabeth provided Lynn with considerable leverage in their relationship. Leverage that she used to gain acceptance from her husband for her own two-year love relationship with Joan, a work colleague, which she had kept hidden up to that point

And so Elizabeth became a part of the du Preez family. Lydia never returned to claim her child and, although Lynn attempted to contact her on several occasions, the telephone number she had left was disconnected and Lynn had no other way of contacting her. Lynn began to realise how little she had actually known about the woman who had lived in their home for over five years, despite her liberal beliefs. She vaguely recalled Lydia mentioning a sick mother living in the Eastern Cape Province, but she had no contact details for her and, for all she knew, the woman could have died in the interim.

Lynn and Barry paid the necessary bribes to register Elizabeth as their own child, which was never thereafter questioned as Elizabeth's skin was so light. Peace returned to the du Preez household.

As Elizabeth grew up, she gradually became aware that her relationship with her mother was not like that of most other girls. Lynn provided all the physical requirements, education and intellectual stimulation, but never any affection or love. However, she instilled in Elizabeth a powerful sense of her own abilities and in her strength as a woman. Barry doted on Elizabeth but he remained married to his work and she saw very little of him. But, when she did, he provided her with love and attention and affirmation.

Elizabeth was provided with the best education that the du Preez's could afford and she completed a degree in commerce, followed by an MBA at South Africa's top business school. By twenty-eight, Elizabeth was employed as a Management Consultant at a prestigious firm, was putting in eighty-hour work weeks and was earning a salary well in advance of most of her peers. By thirty-five Elizabeth was already a junior partner and well on her way to being offered a partnership before she was forty. And then her troubles began.

One night, as she was preparing for bed, after a long, gruelling day spent compiling a management report for a large mining company; Elizabeth felt a strange flutter in her chest. Thinking that it was merely a touch of heartburn after weeks spent subsisting on greasy cafeteria food, or else anxiety at the prospect of presenting the (mostly) bad news at the management meeting with the client the following day, Elizabeth decided to make herself a cup of camomile tea. But, as the water was boiling, she began to feel steadily worse and worse. She was suddenly overwhelmed by a sense of dread that was completely out of all proportion to the meeting that lay ahead the following day. She felt so restless and anxious that she could hardly stand still for long enough to pour the tea.

Elizabeth began to pace up-and-down in the confined space of her kitchen. Her heart was pounding in her ribcage and the blood was booming in her ears. It felt as if she was clinging to her sanity with her fingernails; as if she was but a single breath away from losing all control. She was gripped by a sudden urge to run away, as fast and as far as she possibly could. But where to run to?

It began to feel as if the walls of the kitchen were closing in on her, suffocating her, and Elizabeth threw open the door and rushed outside into the small, dark garden, where she bent over, her hands on her knees, gasping for air. Nothing was obstructing her airway and yet she felt as if she could not breathe. Nothing was wrong with her heart and yet she felt as if it might, at any moment, and without warning, stop. A cold sweat broke upon Elizabeth's brow and a wave of nausea had her retching and gasping. And then the dread inside forced her to start pacing again. Up-and-down she paced, backwards-and-forwards along the garden path, gulping and gasping and sobbing, the blood in her veins pumping pure, icy terror, as the perspiration dripped from her body.

Eventually, gradually, the feeling abated and Elizabeth finally fell asleep at two am, only to be awakened by her alarm at five am. She had a plane to catch and a presentation to get through.

In the cold light of morning, it was difficult to imagine exactly what the problem had been. But, shortly after the plane had taken off and the seatbelt lights had been extinguished, Elizabeth began to feel the beginnings of the panic of the previous night starting to lick at her mind. Only this time she was in a plane at thirty thousand feet, with her work colleagues in the adjacent row of seats!

Elizabeth jumped out of her seat and rushed to the toilets where she barricaded herself for the next ten minutes, breathing deeply and focussing all of her attention on jiggling her leg up and down. This tactic seemed to enable her to control her emotions and within a few minutes her panic had passed. But Elizabeth knew that she had to get help, and fast.

The day passed in a blur and Elizabeth auto-piloted the presentation. The first moment she was able, Elizabeth called to set up an emergency appointment with her doctor the following day.

Even after extensive tests Elizabeth's doctor was unable to find anything physically wrong with her. He eventually referred her to a psychiatrist, who prescribed anti-depressants and recommended that Elizabeth see a psychologist to talk through the underlying psychological issues associated with panic attacks.

Elizabeth visited the psychologist twice a week for six months, during which time she was able to deal with a number of outstanding issues from her childhood. Issues such as high, often unrealistic, performance expectations, combined with a lack of love and attention from her mother and her mostly absent father. The psychologist used cognitive behavioural therapy to help Elizabeth to learn through her own experience, in a safe and repetitive manner, that her panic symptoms were not life threatening. The panic attacks began to resolve and Elizabeth stopped fearing flying or other potential trigger events. Her life was gradually returning to normal.

But during the time that Elizabeth was seeing the psychologist, she began experiencing extremely vivid dreams at night. Later, she began having daytime flashes of memories that certainly weren't her own. These were powerful images of experiences she had never had; of people she was certain she had never met; and of places she had never visited. It was most disconcerting, and often actually terrifying, and so Elizabeth began reading intensively about people who had had similar experiences in their lives. She gradually became convinced that she was having flashbacks to previous lives that she had lived. The level of vivid detail she could recall could simply not be explained away by imagination or dim memories of movies or books she had read.

Elizabeth told her psychologist about her theory that these were memories from past lives. The psychologist had had several patients in the past who had presented with similar concerns, and, despite his own conflicting spiritual beliefs, he referred Elizabeth to Sarah Kavanaugh, a colleague of his.

Sarah Cavanaugh was not at all what Elizabeth had expected. When Elizabeth's psychologist had mentioned that Sarah was a trained shaman, in addition to being a psychologist and a hypnotherapist, Elizabeth had anticipated that Sarah would be dressed in tie-dyed clothing and leather sandals and would be burning incense. However Sarah's office looked like a typical psychologist's office, with framed certificates on the wall, shelves full of weighty academic tomes and dark, sombre furnishings. Sarah herself was conservatively dressed in a sober navy-blue suit and white shirt, with her steel-grey hair in a severe, short style. She looked far more like a banker than a shaman. Her manner was brisk and matter-of-fact.

"Elizabeth, your panic attacks are a sure sign that there is something deep within your psyche that needs to be addressed. I understand that the anti-depressants and the therapy thus far have enabled you to cope with the symptoms and to learn to manage your condition. However, we need to address the deep-seated issues if we want to achieve complete healing.

Any physical or psychological pain we experience is a blessing because it shows us where we need to work. Instead of avoiding or running away from pain, we need to move towards it so as to discover what it has to teach us.

Thus far you have simply engaged in a palliative approach or, at the minimum, in addressing surface issues from your current life as Elizabeth. Now we need to start addressing the real, deep issues from previous lives, so as to ensure deep healing of the spirit and the raising of your consciousness to the next level, for which you are clearly now becoming ready, as evidenced by your pain.

Each lifetime is set up to hold certain lessons. Before every incarnation there is a process of choosing the parents, the significant partners, the situations and the challenges that will enable the being to experience what it needs in order to learn what it wishes to teach itself. Some of these lessons are obvious and relatively quick and easy to learn. Mostly these are the lessons that span only the one lifetime.

And then there are the more complicated lessons that can span several lifetimes. Often these are the lessons that cause us the most pain and difficulty in an individual life. You and I are going to go on a voyage of discovery together. We are going to find all of your lifetimes in which there are outstanding, unresolved issues and we are going to resolve those issues. This process will free you to fully become all that you were meant to be in this lifetime.

There are absolutely no mistakes, Elizabeth. You and I have a contract that was set up pre-incarnationally that, when you were ready, we would meet, in order for me to assist you in this way."

Elizabeth felt a great weight lifting from her mind at Sarah's words. She was beginning to feel more confident that this was the right path for her to follow and Sarah's manner inspired complete honesty:

"*Sarah, this is all very strange to me. Since my first panic attack, six months ago, it feels as if I have been living in the twilight zone! I've never believed in past-lives. I'm an atheist, for goodness sake! And I always thought that hypnosis was something done by stage magicians to entertain people! But since I have started experiencing these vivid memories, I'm not sure of anything anymore. Some of the memories are so disturbing that I'm finding it difficult to function properly at my job. I just want this stuff to go away so that I can continue with my normal life. That's why, at this point, I'm willing to try anything that promises to help.*"

"*Elizabeth, I'm not sure that your life will ever return to what it was before the panic attacks. I'm not sure that's even in your best interests. But we will seek, and attain, healing for your spirit through this process. That is what you are meant to do at this point in your journey and it is the most important job you currently have. So, without further ado, let's get started.*"

Sarah asked Elizabeth to lie down on the comfortable couch in her office and covered her with a light blanket as she asked Elizabeth to close her eyes and to relax. She invoked the protection of Elizabeth's higher self and her guides, as well as the protection of Sarah's own higher self and guides. This she did to ensure that no psychic or energy leeches would be picked up during the journey that they would now be embarking upon together.

Then she proceeded to induce within Elizabeth a state of deep relaxation using successively deepening breathing exercises and visual imagery. The process was designed to transition Elizabeth's brainwaves from the beta wave pattern of normal consciousness to alpha brainwaves, which are typical of a sleeping or meditative state. For Elizabeth it merely felt as if she were in an unaccustomed state of deep relaxation.

Once Elizabeth was completely relaxed, Sarah made her aware of the chakra energy centres in her body. From the base chakra to the crown chakra, one-by-one, Sarah instructed Elizabeth to open and clear these energy centres. She focussed specifically on the third-eye chakra in the centre of Elizabeth's forehead, between her eyes, and also on opening her heart chakra. With the third-eye chakra open, it would be far easier for Elizabeth to access the experiences that she needed to heal, and with her heart chakra open, Elizabeth would remain in connection with her higher self, which would guide the process. Then Sarah asked Elizabeth to go directly to the place where she most needed to find healing and resolution.

For a moment Elizabeth found herself drifting along in quiet, peaceful darkness and then, suddenly, her nostrils were assailed by a powerfully unpleasant and momentarily unfamiliar odour. In an instant, Elizabeth found herself immersed in an incredibly vivid, intensely emotional scene and she gasped in astonishment. Although this was certainly no memory from Elizabeth's current life, she recognised this scene from her recurring dreams! But her dreams had definitely never been this real and immersive. For a moment Elizabeth was overwhelmed by the experience and completely lost her sense of the room in which she lay.

Then, Sarah's voice recalled Elizabeth to her quest for self-healing, *"Elizabeth, where are you? Describe to me what you can see."*

"I'm on a battlefield. I can smell the stench of cordite and blood and fear. Everywhere, wounded and dying men are screaming and horses are neighing. There's smoke and snow

obscuring my vision. This is utter chaos! My shoulder... I'm badly wounded; my right arm and shoulder are completely useless! My horse... where's my horse? I've been injured and I'm off my horse. Where's my sword? There... lying on the ground is a sabre. It's not mine, it's much shorter and curved, but I pick it up anyway with my left hand. It's the sabre of the dying soldier on the ground before me, arterial blood gushing from a deep neck wound. Oh wait, I've got it wrong - I did that to him, and with this sword! I killed that man with his own sword!

I hear someone behind me. I turn around. An infantryman! He's got a short sword. Before he can attack, I run him through with my borrowed sabre, using my left hand. And then there's another to my left. He's dead before he can even think of attacking me! Even with my left hand, I'm so much better than this Russian rabble! I look around. Now where's my horse? I need to get back on my horse and get my men back behind the line, as ordered. A sudden blur of movement to my right and I turn to confront another attacker, but then suddenly it all goes black. What's happened? Where am I? Where's my horse?"

"Elizabeth, I want you to lift your consciousness up. Lift up to a vantage point above this battlefield and tell me what you see."

"There I am – I've just disabled my attacker. I pull my sword free and then I hear a whinnying behind me. I turn around... and there! There's my horse! It rears up in panic and lands. Oh my God! My horse has landed with one of its hooves right in the middle of my chest. My chest is completely crushed! There's blood coming out of my mouth and nostrils. I'm dying! I'm dead - killed by my own horse! I'm furious. What an ignoble way to die! I was a much better fighter than *all of them and yet I was killed by my very own horse. I didn't even make it to the end of the battle. I wasn't able to lead my men back behind the line. All my training, all my experience, all my hopes and dreams and ambitions... all for nothing."*

"OK, Elizabeth, let's leave the battle field now. Is there anything else in this lifetime you need to see?"

After a long pause, during which Elizabeth's inner-vision recalibrated, she continued, "*I'm in a large, luxuriously appointed room. There's a four-poster bed with heavy, embroidered, brocade draperies. I'm feeling very excited. There she is - my little cousin. Marie-Claire. She's ten but, although I'm only two years older, I'm much bigger and stronger than her. She's terrified of me and it makes me feel even more excited and powerful. She's on the bed, backing away from me; her legs kicking at me in a mass of frilly white petticoats. I grab hold of her chubby legs and pull her towards me. She's kicking and screaming and I grab her and clamp my hand over her mouth. Her eyes roll back in terror. I can't believe how excited this makes me feel! This is even better than I ever could have imagined!*

I pinch Marie-Claire hard on her arm, twisting her soft flesh between my fingers and thumb and she moans loudly and tries to bite my hand that is covering her mouth. Then I slap her across her face several times and she looks up at me, gasping with shock. I hold her down with one hand across her neck while my other hand explores beneath her petticoats. I've always wondered what a girl would feel like and now I'm finally getting to find out. I feel her soft, smooth thighs and my excitement grows. Today I'll satisfy both my curiosity and my desire for revenge.

Just then Marthe calls out in the passage and Marie-Claire kicks away from me and rolls off the far side of the bed.

She charges out of the door and into the passage, desperately calling for Marthe. Damn! I'll have to make another opportunity to further my explorations."

"And, do you get another opportunity?"

"No. I see Marie-Claire's family leaving. They are getting into their coach. I am looking from my window. From behind the curtains. Not wanting to be seen. I have been banished to my room. I am hurt. Oh... that's right, I have been beaten. Severely beaten. I can see that now. I am in my father's study. He doesn't even want to talk to me. He is furious; angrier than I have ever seen him. And now he is beating me with his cane. Twelve strokes. With all of his strength. Now I'm locked up in my room. It's been almost two weeks of bread and water and boredom and I'm slowly going insane. Now I'm leaving for the military academy. My father doesn't even say goodbye..."

"Elizabeth, do you have any further memories from this lifetime?"

Elizabeth was quiet for a moment and then she replied, *"My men tell me that the prisoner has been readied for me and so I descend the steps and into the stone passageway beneath the kitchens. The walls are lit with torches. I enter the room and there he is. The poacher! He is dressed only in leather breeches, his upper body glistening with sweat and fresh blood running down his face in the candlelight. I gag him with a filthy rag and his eyes widen in fear as I slowly smile, allowing him to see my excitement. There is a very intimate relationship between the victim and the perpetrator, isn't there? I'll take my time exacting my revenge and then I'll take my time despatching him to his maker. There will be no consequences resulting from this act, as this is my property and he is merely a peasant, and a thief.*

Fair game, as it were! I become increasingly aroused as I slowly check the sharpness of my knife blade. Actually I know it's exactly as sharp as I need it to be; I'm just playing with my prey. I make eye contact with my plaything and I relish the metallic tang of fear in the air. I'm going to enjoy this..."

"All right, Elizabeth, let's leave that part of the story there. Now I want you to see if you can find the final conclusion to this incarnation. What can you see?"

"*I see a funeral. It's a military funeral with full honours. It's his funeral and he's filled with rage! He believes that he can never move on from here. He is absolutely stuck.*"

"Why is he so angry?"

"*Because this funeral is a farce! He's being buried with full military honours, as if he were a hero, but he died the most ignoble of deaths - killed by his own horse on the battlefield! And he never even got to complete his battle. He who was the top of his class every year in the academy. He who was renowned for his superior horsemanship and his skill with the sword. He who was a veteran of so many campaigns! It's a travesty! This whole life was about forcing others to respect and admire him; to feel jealous of him; to fear him. He had no real love and so he decided to ensure that he had the next best thing - respect and fear - in abundance.*"

"Elizabeth, bring yourself, your present self as the personality Elizabeth, into the presence of this being. What do you have to say to him?"

Without a moment's hesitation, Elizabeth said, "*I will complete the battle for you.*"

"What do you mean by that, Elizabeth?"

"*His battle was to find love. Or, at least, the only substitutes for love that he believed he could get. But what he really needed to find was self-love. He sought outside of himself for that which he would only be able to find within. And that inward search has been the journey for me of this lifetime. I have had to seek, and eventually find, deep within myself, true self-love. So, in this way, I complete his journey for him."*

"OK, you're doing great, Elizabeth. What is he doing now?"

"For the first time in his life, ever, he is crying. He understands what I am saying to him. It all makes sense to him now. He can finally move on."

"Elizabeth, I want you to bring this being into your heart. Let him reside there in the love that he has craved for his entire existence. Now, I want you to take three deep breaths and release on each out-breath this entire lifetime and any attachments that remain. Just let it all go. Breathe...breathe...breathe.

Now, is there anything remaining from this lifetime that needs to be addressed? No... OK, then let's bring you back to normal consciousness."

Elizabeth was extremely shaken by her first experience with Sarah. The images she had seen whilst under hypnosis had been so incredibly vivid. She had felt as if she were truly there on that battlefield, experiencing the full assault to her senses of the battle. Elizabeth was absolutely certain that there was no way she could have conjured up such a powerful experience in her own imagination. She was starting to become convinced that there really was something to these past-life experiences and she was actually looking forward to her next session with Sarah.

However, by the time that Elizabeth next saw Sarah, she had had time to think about what she had experienced and she had several questions.

"Sarah, I've been having some difficulty processing what happened during last week's session. The being that I encountered under hypnosis was just such a terrible person. I simply can't believe that I would ever do the horrible things that he did. And, if I start to think that I did, then I find myself feeling immense guilt and shame for things that I didn't even know that I had done before last week!"

"Elizabeth, you didn't do those things. He did. Just as the lifetime, from which you experienced flashes under hypnosis last week, is like a set of clothing worn by your higher self for a limited time, just so is Elizabeth another set of clothing. You are judging what a soldier did over two centuries ago from the perspective of your current lifetime and it simply cannot be judged from that perspective. In fact, it cannot be judged at all. Merely observed with compassion, just as you would wish all of your own so-called mistakes to be observed with compassion. Each and every life that you encounter, whether your own past-lives or the lives of other beings, are each just an expression of God. Each being you encounter is God, and the things that people do are simply the expressions of God under that specific set of circumstances. Human judgements are not God's judgements.

You, from the perspective of Elizabeth, cannot understand the full meaning and impact of any life, not even your own current incarnation. When you are done with incarnating, all of this will make much more sense. Until then, simply observe with compassion."

"But... was I really an officer in Napoleon's army in a previous life or not? It simply doesn't make sense to me!"

"*You're feeling frustrated and it's because you are insisting upon things being either true or false. You are insisting upon there being only one, objective truth, whereas all truth is really subjective and temporary. What is true from one perspective is not true from another. All of it is just stories. Your own life is simply a story that you are telling yourself about yourself. You thread together your memories, beliefs and current experiences in such a way that it forms a coherent story that you tell yourself.*

Is the story true? Well, a better question would be - is the story useful? Does it allow you to develop and grow as a spiritual being? Does it allow you to elevate your consciousness? If so, then it's a useful story. So, now I ask you - is the story of the lifetime we encountered last week a useful story?"

"*Well, it did allow me to understand my life-long search for self-love and self-acceptance within a broader context. It allowed me to find meaning in my love-less relationship with my mother and in my ego-drive to achieve and to always be "the best". So, yes, I suppose it is a very useful story.*"

"*Well, then. There's your answer. For myself, I'm not really interested in whether these are actually stories of past lives or the wild imaginings of some extremely creative part of your mind! Of far greater interest to me is why, out of an infinity of possible stories, these specific stories are the ones that are arising for you. Clearly there is great meaning and value in these stories and it's our job to discover that value together in order to bring about healing.*

So, let's see if we can unearth any more useful stories this week, shall we?"

The Green Lady fell silent and waited for me to ask the question that was quivering on my lips.

"*It seems as if Elizabeth was struggling with exactly the same issue that has been a challenge for me! She too needed to be told about the simultaneous importance of story and of not holding too tightly to story.*"

My companion smiled at me, "*Well, yes, of course. This is why I am able to assist you in your difficulties in this regard. I too have experienced the same struggle. And the wisdom that passed through Sarah Cavanaugh to Elizabeth passes again through me to you. In time it will pass on through you to someone else who needs it; perhaps in the pages of the book you will write! There are no mistakes and we meet, and interact with, the people we do for a reason. Many meetings are, in fact, pre-planned before we even incarnate into these lifetimes. What may seem like random events from the perspective of the incarnated personality may be extremely meaningful and important from the perspective of the indwelling spirit.*

But, for now, I'd like you to reflect on these thoughts for the time we are apart and we will continue the story of Elizabeth next week."

Chapter 8:
Weaving Together the
Threads (part 2)

Sarah repeated the hypnotic induction of the previous week and this time, because she knew what to expect, Elizabeth was able to much more rapidly achieve a state of deep relaxation. When Sarah asked her to go to the place which most required healing, she instantly found herself inside of another powerfully emotional and vividly realistic scene. It didn't feel like a memory at all. She was right there, right at that very moment. Although the experience was every bit as intense as the previous session with Sarah, this time Elizabeth was able to retain a part of her consciousness as an observer so as to engage in the process of healing. It definitely became easier when one knew what to expect of the process.

"Elizabeth, where are you? Describe to me what you see."

"I'm sitting on a stair made of polished black granite. I'm very tired, scared, lonely and missing my family. I don't know where I am and I have no idea of how I'll ever get back home again. On my lap is a small, earthenware bowl, decorated with brightly painted ethnic swirls and patterns. I know that this is something very precious to me and I hold tightly onto it.

As I observe richly-dressed people walking up-and-down the stairs, either glaring at me or observing me with pity, I start to feel deeply ashamed. I'm dressed in such plain, tatty clothing and my hair is a ratty mess, in comparison to their oiled and coiffed locks. My bare feet are filthy. I feel totally out of place and I have no idea of what is going to happen to me. A merchant bearing a tray of highly polished silverware walks past and sneers at me. As I glance down once more at the bowl in my lap, I suddenly realise how very shabby it is. How inferior in comparison to the brilliantly polished and expensive bowls that I can see on the tray. And so I hide it in a fold of my grubby robe. A loud cawing startles me and I jump to my feet, accidentally dropping my bowl. It rolls down the stairs and smashes on the hard ground below. The big, black bird watches me with its head to one side as tears begin to roll down my dirty cheeks," Elizabeth remained silent for several moments as the memory faded, but the feeling of sadness persisted.

"*Can you share any further memories from this lifetime, Elizabeth?*" Sarah prompted her again.

Once more there was a pause as Elizabeth's perspective shifted. And then she said, "*I'm watching my sister dancing around the fire. It's the dance of the story of our people. The story my Nanni told me when I was little. Lemma! She's so beautiful, so powerful and in control as she moves her body to the rhythm of the chanting. She's all grown-up and her body is unrecognisable to me as that of my childhood friend. I look down at my own flat chest and skinny legs and I feel more than a little bit jealous of her. Then I feel sad that she will be leaving me so soon. Nanni whispers to me, 'Didu, someday it will be you,' and then I begin to feel* proud and a little bit scared. How will I ever be able to dance like that?

Sarah, I think this happened before the previous memory I shared."

"Anything else?" asked Sarah.

"I'm just drifting now... drifting quietly in the darkness. Wait. The darkness is beginning to resolve into a scene. Here I am. Oh, now I am grown-up. I didn't have to worry! My body is that of a fully grown woman. I'm in a place dimly lit with candles; the sound of chanting echoing off the walls and off the high ceiling. I'm in the temple with the other adepts. Today I will die to my old life and be born into my new life. I know that great power and wealth and privilege lie within my grasp. This is everything I ever wanted! Everything I worked for. I am elated and also terrified because I know that if my secret was to be revealed, I would not only lose all my privilege, but would also be executed for treason. A small part of me almost wishes that would happen because I feel so ashamed for betraying my upbringing and my people. Another part of me feels vindicated that a simple, so-called inferior girl could so successfully infiltrate the highest echelons of power of the enemies of my people.

Such conflicted feelings! Wanting to belong and yet, at the same time, despising that to which I seek admittance. Most of all, at the very deepest levels, I feel hatred of myself. I know myself to be deeply unworthy. No-one would accept me or want me if I didn't constantly lie about who I really am. The person I truly am is acceptable to none; least of all to myself."

"Is there anything more that you can see, Elizabeth?"

"No, the scene has dissolved and I am floating once more in a quiet, dark and peaceful place. I can't say that I'm sorry to let that experience go. Those were some very unpleasant emotions. Guilt and shame and anger and hatred. But, most of all, deep, deep sadness."

"*How does this lifetime end, Elizabeth?*" asked Sarah.

"*Fire falling from the sky! I've seen this before. When I was little more than a child. Oh! That's how I managed to infiltrate their school and receive what was my due. But now the fiery rocks are destroying the temple. Around me lie scattered the broken bodies of my fellow priests and priestesses. The ancient embroidered temple curtains are a wall of flames. The entrance has caved in. I frantically look around me in panic. I'm trapped! Can nobody help me? Peer! Peer, where are you now when I need you the most? Peer, help me! Help us! Get me out of here! If I die, then you die too, remember? Then another loud crash, a harsh metallic taste in my mouth and everything fades to black...*"

"*Elizabeth, bring yourself into the presence of Peer. Peer, what do you have to say to me?*"

Elizabeth suddenly became aware of the presence of another being inside her own mind: "*I guess you've discovered my guilty little secret! I'm still here; I'm still with Elizabeth. I was never released when Didu died, as her death was so sudden. Normally the priests and priestesses would be given prior warning of their impending death and would have ample time to revoke the contract with their Peer. I chose not to provide Didu with a warning that her end was nigh and so I was able to stay on. I wanted to experience more lifetimes associated with this being. It worked out really well for me. Her next lifetime, as an officer in Napoleon's army, was a simply glorious experience for me!*"

"*Peer, have you ever been incarnated into a physical form yourself?*"

"No, that's simply too risky for me. I prefer not to forget what I am. But I can experience the full spectrum of experiences I wish to have by partnering with incarnated beings who allow me access. This works very well for me!"

"Peer, that might well be so, but your time with this being, currently known as Elizabeth, has come to an end. Right now we are going to release you to whatever it is that lies ahead for you on your path.

Elizabeth, listen to me now. I want you to cast a net made of bright, white light and trap Peer in that net. He can't escape from your net. OK, tell me what Peer is doing now?"

"He's just sitting there, trapped in the net."

"Good. Now Peer, tell me what you're still doing in Elizabeth's consciousness? You don't belong here!"

"Of course I do! I was invited here. There was a contract that was willingly entered into by both parties."

"Peer, tell me about that contract."

"I provided the woman, Didu, with knowledge and information which I was able to bring through the Veil of Forgetting. She used this information to gain access to the highest echelons of power. She had virtually unlimited wealth and power and influence. She became the High Priestess - the highest position of all, due to me!"

"What did you get in return, Peer?"

"Well, my name says it all! I became her peer; her equal. This was an equal partnership, you know. This is how we did it in that time and place. I was able to experience life as an incarnated being through her. She undertook to be my host in exchange for the powers and knowledge that I granted her. By prompting and encouraging her to engage in dark sexual practises, cruelty, violence, torture and other perversions of power, I was also able to feed on the fear, pain

and other negative energies associated with these practices. I did this in several of her other lifetimes too. Jean-Philippe, in particular, was an extremely exciting lifetime for me. He was naturally inclined to engage in violence and sexual perversion and needed little encouragement from me to do so. In fact, he wasn't even aware of my presence at all! His need to forcefully command respect and fear from all those he encountered gave me ample opportunity for feeding. What a glorious lifetime that was for me! In fact, this entire partnership has been very satisfying for me!"

"*Why do you need to feed, Peer? You are discarnate. You do not have a body?*"

And when Peer next spoke, Elizabeth could feel something unexpected from him. What was that? Loss? Sadness? Perhaps even shame?

"*I... we... that is to say those of us who agree to these contracts... we have lost our light. We do not have our own source within us. We do not know how to find our own sustenance within ourselves. We are of this duality, just as those of you who incarnate are. But we do not wish to incarnate. We do not wish to experience the deep forgetting. So this is the only way to gain energetic sustenance. To feed. Otherwise, I fear, I shall simply fade away.*"

"*Peer, this contract has come to an end. Didu made that contract and she should have closed that contract before she died, but she didn't, due to the circumstances of her death. So now Elizabeth and I will close the contract. You no longer belong here. You need to evolve your own consciousness and move on.*"

"*Please! Do not cast me out! How will I sustain myself?*"

"Peer, you need to seek help. Perhaps you need to incarnate. But you are not my client. Elizabeth is. And it is apparent that this contract serves neither her, nor the highest good. Peer, on behalf of Elizabeth, I hereby revoke any and all contracts entered into between the two of you, at any time whatsoever.

Elizabeth, I want you to focus on taking three deep breaths and on each out-breath, I want you to breathe Peer out into the column of light in front of you. Release him and let him go. Breathe... breathe... breathe.

Is Peer gone, Elizabeth?"

"Yes, he's gone now. Sarah, what's happening to me? I'm shaking all over!"

"It's OK, Elizabeth. When such a large psychic parasite is removed, there is always a bit of a shock to your energetic body. Just keep breathing deeply and I will ground you. Focus on my hands holding your feet. Stay calm and steady. That's right. You're absolutely fine now."

"Elizabeth, now that you're feeling calm and centred, I want you to return to Didu. Bring her into your mind and say what you need to say to her."

"Didu, you were always enough. You didn't need to become someone else in order to be loved and accepted. You made a mistake - who you truly are is enough. Similarly, who I truly am is enough."

"Very good, Elizabeth. Let's return you to normal consciousness now."

Once Elizabeth had regained her composure and was sitting once more on the sofa, she had a multitude of questions for Sarah.

"Sarah, what just happened here? That was just crazy! How can I believe that I had some kind of... what?

Psychic parasite attached to me! This is just too much to accept! What have you done to me? What insane thoughts and memories have you put into my head?"

"Stay calm, Elizabeth. Remember, these are just stories. And they're not my stories; they're your stories. These are the stories that have arisen in your own consciousness, bearing their gifts for you.

It is, however, so that many people have some form of psychic parasite or another. These are discarnate beings that attach themselves to their human hosts and feed off of their energies. Not all people have an incarnation in which they actively welcomed the entrance of such a parasite into their energy. But we do unconsciously and unwittingly invite them in many other ways, such as through sex with contaminated persons of lower energy, or when our resources are depleted such as when we have a bad illness or by taking drugs, alcohol or in certain places of low energy vibrations. One even needs to be quite careful when meditating to ensure that you provide yourself with simple psychic protection so as to remain immune to these little energy leeches. It's a good idea to practise spiritual hygiene at all times and to rid yourself of any energy leeches from time to time. I can definitely teach you how to do that. But all this is just a story, remember. Tell me, was this story useful?"

"Well... OK, yes... it was useful, I guess. This story tells me that I don't have to try and be something I'm not in order to gain love and acceptance. The person I am is more than enough and I can find all the love I need within myself.

But, if I accept all that, then it starts to become silly to keep trying to find respect and recognition through my career. Why don't I just seek for who I truly am and simply express that? But... where does that leave me in my career?"

"Where indeed? Lots to think about. I'll see you again next week. Try to remain calm and centred, Elizabeth, you're doing exceptionally well."

Chapter 9:
Life Between Lives

Elizabeth arrived at Sarah's consulting rooms in a state of considerable agitation the following week. She was not at all her usual well-groomed self. Her hair was awry and her make-up smudged and she was sporting a large pimple on her previously immaculate chin. She looked scattered and frazzled and nothing at all like the well-groomed business woman who had first entered Sarah's consulting rooms some weeks earlier. Elizabeth had scarcely seated herself before she burst out with, *"Sarah, I'm not sure that this hypnotherapy stuff is doing me any good at all! My life is coming apart at the seams. I'm not able to focus at work any more. It all just seems so silly and trivial. I mean, do these companies really need to be paying me these enormous sums of money to tell them what to do? Am I really doing anything of lasting value? Is what I'm doing meaningful in any way? It's all just about money and somehow I can't find it within myself to be excited about money and possessions any more. What am I doing that makes a lasting, positive difference in the world? What am I doing that makes me feel happy and fulfilled? This was my dream job that I worked so hard to get, and keep, and now I find it utterly boring and ridiculously trivial! What must I do?"*

Sarah answered in a calm and soothing voice, *"Elizabeth, you are asking yourself all the right questions. You are right in the middle of birthing a new you into this reality. And, as with all births, there will be pain and confusion and some fear. You will lose some things and gain others. But, know this, Elizabeth. You are doing the work of your soul. You are finally doing the work that you came to this place to do. You say that your job feels meaningless and trivial. Well, this work we are doing together is the most meaningful and important work you have ever done in your life; in fact, in all of your lifetimes!"*

"What! The work I came to do was to make up silly stories about soldiers and ancient alien civilisations and discarnate energy leeches and..." Elizabeth shook her head, unable to continue, as tears of impotent rage, fear and frustration began to course down her cheeks.

"No, Elizabeth. You deliberately misunderstand me because you are feeling shaken out of the carefully-constructed prison of your ego-mind and it feels deeply uncomfortable. You want to rush back in and slam the door shut behind you. But this is not what your soul wants you to do. It is time for you to awaken to the power of your divine, limitless self. And, if to accomplish that you need to tell yourself some "silly" stories, then so be it.

Let me share a little secret with you. Elizabeth, you do not fear that these stories are silly and trivial. What you actually fear is your power and your magnificence. What you fear is releasing your illusions of your own powerlessness and victim-hood. What you fear is to stand upright in the light of your own higher self and become, finally, who you truly are; an immortal creator being of infinite power!

Well, be courageous, Elizabeth. And know that if the stories really are silly and trivial, then they will have no impact whatsoever on your life. But clearly they are not trivial, as their impact on your life appears to be massive, even after just two sessions."

"I know, I know. But I just feel so confused. This is almost worse than the panic attacks!" wailed Elizabeth.

"Hang in there, it will get better, I promise. And there's no turning back now, so we might as well keep moving forward, wouldn't you say? Now, let's see what work lies ahead for us today. Lie down and let me take you to a place of deep relaxation..."

"Elizabeth, tell me what you see."

"I'm in a very strange place. I'm not in a physical form, but rather in a non-embodied form. I don't think this actually is a lifetime... Oh, right. This is a time between lifetimes. It is the time of review and of choosing the circumstances of the next lifetime. My guide, Michael, is with me. We are discussing what happened in the past two lifetimes, both as Didu and as Jean-Philippe."

"Walk me through the discussion, Elizabeth. You have returned here for a reason. There must be something that you wish to show yourself by coming to this place."

"Michael, I feel so ashamed of what I did in my lifetimes as Didu and as Jean-Philippe. As Didu I betrayed my people, my culture and my upbringing. I became just like our enemies. In fact, I became worse than our enemies because I should have known better, having witnessed and experienced their oppression of my people. I mean, they killed my own mother and grandmother!

I was so driven by fear - the fear of lack, the fear of being discovered to be a fraud, the fear of not being good enough - that I betrayed everything that I should have held most dear. In fact, I betrayed myself too!"

"My dear young friend, you must remember that we chose to set up this lifetime with all of its challenges and circumstances. Everything that happened was perfectly arranged to allow you to experience certain things. The lack of a mother growing up and your admiration for, and secret jealousy of, your brilliant elder sister, for example, set you up perfectly with a burning desire to excel in all things so as to gain the attention and love you felt was lacking in your life, despite the best efforts of your grandmother."

"Yes, it's true. Although she was very loving to us, I always felt that Nanni had so many other responsibilities to take care of in the raising of six children that she didn't have the time and energy for me. Even when she spent time with me, there were always other children present to listen to her stories. I never felt like I was special to her or, in fact, to anyone."

"It was, indeed, quite unusual to be raised by your own grandmother, along with other children, even if she was a child-raising specialist. Normally this would never have happened. A Lemurian child was almost never raised by someone in their own family. It was inevitable that tensions would arise. Of course, this was no mistake. It was part of the set-up conditions of this lifetime.

And then, just as you had been chosen to be trained in the mystery school, just as all your dreams were about to come true and you felt special for the very first time, you were kidnapped. That was a very traumatic experience that caused you to see the world in a completely different light, was it not?"

"Absolutely true. I saw how the Atlanteans lived. They had so much more than my people had ever had. They were surrounded by luxury and beauty and excess and suddenly everything I had been taught to hold dear seemed small and shabby and second-rate.

Then followed two terrible years of abuse and neglect and lack, when all around me was excess to which I was not entitled. And so, when unexpected circumstances made it possible for me to access some of that luxury for myself, I leapt at the chance. In the beginning, just to be able to eat my fill at every meal was worth the subterfuge required!

As I grew up and realised that I was one of the best at the lessons; that I was, for the first time ever, considered special and worthy; well, I guess it just fed my ego and I wanted more and more. I didn't even hesitate when it came to inviting Peer to enter my being in exchange for knowledge and additional power. I wanted all the power I could possibly get! I never wanted to feel like a powerless victim, ever again."

"All this was planned. You were able, in this lifetime, to begin to explore the consequences of living a life from the ego, instead of from the heart. You were able to experience the feeling of being special and "better than" those around you and to know something of the loneliness and isolation, underpinned by fear, that this way of being brings."

"Michael, I know that I allowed my ego to take control in Didu's life and then, in my lifetime as Jean-Philippe, I really allowed my ego to run rampant! I committed some egregious acts: I raped and murdered and tortured people. How do I ever forgive myself for what I did?"

"Young one, although it is true that you did cause considerable harm to others in your lifetimes as both Didu and Jean-Philippe, you must remember that those you harmed had

contracted with you pre-incarnationally to experience being victims to your perpetrator. You have also had several lives in which you played the role of victim. In fact, you have a few lives ahead of you in which you will, once again, be a victim of sorts.

Remember, also, that many of the lusts both Didu and Jean-Philippe experienced were incited by the presence of Peer. Certainly both Didu and Jean-Philippe derived great benefit from Peer. These hungers and drives that he incited helped to mould Jean-Philippe into a powerful and fearless soldier and allowed Didu access to the very highest echelons of power. But his presence was a very mixed blessing indeed and the cost of these powers and knowledge was extremely high for both of these personalities. The cost of accessing inauthentic power is always high, whereas the accessing of authentic power via the heart connection always simplifies and clarifies things for a personality. The heart-connected way of being makes life effortless and in-the-flow.

You will, of course, in another lifetime, have to go to some considerable effort to rid yourself of Peer. But it is planned that you will indeed accomplish this and so Peer will not be a part of your next two lifetimes.

Quite simply, he will not know how to derive benefit from the lives we have planned next. Lives from which he will really not be able to feed. It will do both Peer and yourself well to have him starve, just a little.

Now that you have so fully explored the consequences of two ego-driven lifetimes, next you will be able to explore what happens when the ego is not in charge at all. You will now have a lifetime in which you will begin to seek for an authentic connection, followed by a lifetime in which heart will finally be in charge."

"I'm ready to explore a different way of being, Michael. Let's do it..."

CHAPTER 10:
WEAVING TOGETHER THE
THREADS (PART 3)

" *E*lizabeth, where are you and what are you feeling?"

"I'm in a comfortable, well-furnished room, in front of a fireplace, but I feel like I'm in a dark prison of deepest despair. It feels as if my life is over. Nothing makes sense without her; my art, my life, is worthless and I just want to end it all."

"Who is she and what happened here?"

"Hannah. My love, my heart, the centre of my universe, my muse... Hannah, my everything. She's left me and I don't even know where she went. She's never coming back and my world has ended. On the table in front of me is a loaded pistol. I don't want to be here anymore without her. I just want the pain to end. I'm going to end it all, right now."

"Elizabeth, what happens now?"

"I pick up the gun, put the barrel into my mouth and pull the trigger."

"Can you find an earlier memory from this lifetime, Elizabeth, so we can find out what we're dealing with here?"

"I'm floating in a quiet, dark space now. The pain has ended and I'm feeling more at peace. Oh, this is not a memory *from earlier in this lifetime, but rather a memory from the time after this life had ended."*

"OK, well let's explore that then, Elizabeth. This memory has arisen for a reason. There is something here that holds an important message or lesson for you. Tell me a little more about what you are experiencing now."

"The floating is over and I find myself in the place of life review with my spirit guide, Michael. I sense that Michael and I have done a lot of work together in order for me to reach a place of acceptance of the life that has just ended."

"David, are you now at peace with the way in which your last life ended?"

"Yes, it's taken me some time and I'm very grateful for your love and guidance, Michael. This was a very traumatic way to end a life and I don't think I'll choose suicide again in future lives. I had so many opportunities in this lifetime and yet, by choosing to end this life prematurely, I chose to explore so few of them."

"That is indeed so, David, but you did achieve the main learning of that lifetime. What was that for you?"

"Well, I didn't repeat Jean-Philippe's and Didu's mistake of allowing my ego to run the show. But, equally, I didn't search for my authentic connection to my higher self either. I just drifted along, squandering my gifts and opportunities until I found someone in whom I chose to place my entire reason for being. That the person I chose was hardly worthy wasn't the point. In fact, it was probably a saving grace or I might have decided that it was a good thing to place myself completely at the mercy of another and allow that person to become my entire world."

"Indeed. The being incarnated as Hannah played her role to perfection. What else did you learn?"

"The achievements of the ego are as nothing without the true heart connection to the divine. David's acclaim as an artist dies with him. Even if the artworks live on, the immortal soul finds no value whatsoever in recognition and fame. I definitely felt the lack of a heart connection during David's life, but, instead of searching for that connection within my own heart, I sought it outside of myself and placed it in Hannah. Externalising our power and our OK-ness will never work. We need to find it within ourselves."

"That is correct, David. We can now begin preparing for your next lifetime; a life in which you <u>will</u> find this connection within yourself."

"Elizabeth, before we explore other lives any further, we need to address any outstanding issues from your life as David. Please bring David to stand before you. What do you have to say to him?"

"David, thank you for being willing to learn the hard way that we need to find our own divine connection within. Because you were willing to experience the pain of having your entire reason for being ripped away from you, I didn't have to do that in my current lifetime as Elizabeth. Thanks to the lessons you learnt during your lifetime, I have not externalised my power, my purpose or my sense of self in anyone else. This has stood me in great stead in coping with the challenges of my own lifetime.

Also, the realisation, which I gained from your experiences, that suicide is definitely not the easy way out has meant that I have stayed the course when my own life was challenging and frightening."

"Anything else, Elizabeth?"

"No, I'm at peace with David's life. Whereas before his shoulders were bowed and he looked defeated and ashamed, he is now standing upright and making eye contact with me. I think that this experience has allowed him to find some peace with the lessons of his lifetime."

"That's great, Elizabeth and it's obviously the reason why you had to visit David's lifetime. Now, I want you to bring David into your heart. Allow him to move through the loving, healing portal of your heart into his own divine connection. Take three deep breaths and breathe David through your heart now, Elizabeth. Breathe... breathe...breathe. Has David left now, Elizabeth?"

"Yes, he has... I'm just floating in the peaceful darkness."

"Good, then let's move onto the next place that calls for healing. Allow yourself to be guided by your inner knowing to where you most need to be..."

"Elizabeth, where are you now? Please describe for me what you can see."

"I'm once more at the place between lives. Michael and I are busy discussing my next lifetime. This is where we were before I had the brief interaction with David that has just concluded."

"That's great, Elizabeth. Obviously there is something here that you need to experience. Tell me more about what's going on."

"*Michael, I feel that perhaps the extraordinary talents and abilities I had in my life as David were a distraction for me. I also don't want to have a lifetime in which I am not required to fend for myself. I need to find my way towards standing on my own two feet without having it all handed to me on a platter. I want to find what I require within my own heart.*"

"*Very well, then let us proceed with the design of your next life; a life in which heart will be in charge.*

In your following life, you will not be able to fool yourself that you are in any way better than, or more special than, anyone else. In the next lifetime that you have chosen, you will, in fact, have diminished metal capacity. Not enough that you won't be able to function, but just enough that you won't be able to consider yourself superior to anyone. You will have to find your heart connection and your connection with others from this place of lack.

One very important point that I need you to understand is that this next lifetime is, in no way, punishment for what you did in any of your previous lifetimes. It is merely the set-up conditions which will allow you to have the experiences that your soul requires in order to progress."

"*I understand this, Michael, and I willingly choose this life as a means of furthering the ultimate goals of my soul. Right now it all makes sense and everything is so clear. But it gets a lot more confusing and frightening when I have forgotten once more who I really am and I find myself lost in the illusion of incarnation.*"

"*It is so that beings that choose to incarnate into separation and into forgetting are able to progress very rapidly. But it is also so that this is considered to be a very difficult way of achieving the goals of your spirit. As you know, those beings that do enter into separation are considered to be very courageous and are much sought after later on as their experiences are invaluable in assisting and training others. What an incredible opportunity to see what you will become; what you will create yourself to be; if you forget completely who and what you truly are!"*

"I know that, Michael, and that is why I'm willing to do this. I'm looking forward to seeing how this life will turn out and I'm particularly looking forward to standing here with you at the end of this life and reviewing what happened!"

"Good, then let's get you started..."

Sarah brought Elizabeth out of her hypnotic state and then sat down with her on the couch to discuss the experiences she had just shared.

"Elizabeth, how do you feel about the place you visited in today's session?"

"It was fascinating, actually! That souls will deliberately choose difficult and challenging lifetimes; lifetimes in which they know that they will experience hardship and pain and suffering, just so that they can advance themselves and teach themselves new lessons about themselves... well that's kind of fascinating, and a little difficult to comprehend from our perspective as human beings, isn't it? I mean, as human beings we generally go out of our way to avoid pain and discomfort, don't we?"

"I think that it's difficult to understand these things from within the illusion. But when your soul stands outside of the illusion and you remember once more who you truly are... well... it seems as if it certainly makes a lot more sense then!

What today's session does for me is to bring about
the realisation that there is a purpose to each lifetime. That
our lives are meaningful. Even, or, especially, the hard bits.
That's a comforting thought, don't you think?"

"Yes, I guess it is. It makes it easier for me to accept,
and work through, the challenges I'm experiencing at the
moment. So, what's next, Sarah?"

"Well, that's really up to you! We'll see when we
meet again next week."

"Elizabeth describe for me what you can see right
now."

"Not much really! I'm in a very dark place. I can't
even see my hand in front of my face. I'm terrified that they'll
find me. I'm freezing cold and... Oh yuck! The front of my
pants are cold and wet. Oh! I see. I wet myself when I heard
the shouts of the other children so close to my hiding place.
This is terrible. I feel so lonely and uncomprehending of the
cruelty I encounter daily from my classmates."

"OK, anything else?"

"Well, from my perspective as Elizabeth, I am aware
of the pattern on Rodney's jersey. It's a Fair Isle pattern in
shades of pale blue and green. As I watch, I'm noticing that
the shades in the jersey are steadily getting darker. Oh, wait,
it's Rodney but he's all grown up now. His jersey is now in
shades of brown and olive green. Oh, I see. The patterns,
established in his childhood; the patterns of running away and
hiding from people for fear of being hurt continue, even into
his adulthood. Also the patterns of being lonely and afraid of
being mocked, the incomprehension at how people can be as
cruel and intolerant as they are.

But wait! Now I see something different. Rodney has a friend! It's a little boy. Also an outcast, just as Rodney was when he was a small boy. Rodney's new friend doesn't care that Rodney is slow and that he stutters. He is fascinated by all the knowledge that Rodney can share about the birds and their habits. He watches entranced as Rodney calls the various birds to himself by imitating their calls."

"Is there anything else?"

"Yes, now I see Rodney surrounded by lots of children! He has broken the habits; changed the patterns of a lifetime and he has many friends with whom to share his life and his passion for birds. Rodney is actually popular! But, more importantly, he feels loved and valued for who he truly is."

"Take yourself to the moment of Rodney's death."

"I'm climbing the ladder to check up on the nest. All is fine - there are the three eggs. They should be hatching very soon. Suddenly I feel as if a giant fist has grabbed my heart and I have no breath left. I feel my consciousness move into my heart and then I exit through the hole in my heart and I am free!

I'm free! I'm free and I'm flying with the birds. I'm flying, I'm flying! I'm flying into the light..."

"Elizabeth, bring Rodney to your mind. Have him stand before you and tell him what he needs to hear from you."

"Rodney is standing in front of me now and I'm shining pure love at him from the centre of my heart. It's a beam of brilliant white love-light. Rodney's mouth falls open in awe and astonishment and his eyes are shining. He asks me, 'Are you an angel?' Oh no! That is just so funny... and so sweet!"

Elizabeth began laughing, as tears of joy streamed down her cheeks.

"*No, Rodney, I'm not an angel. I'm really just you in another form. I am you and you are me. Rodney, are you ready to come home?*"

"*Elizabeth, what is Rodney doing right now?*"

"*He's just smiling at me - the biggest, cheesiest grin I've ever seen! And he's nodding his head so hard that I'm afraid it might fall right off!*"

"*Elizabeth, invite Rodney to come home to your heart. Let the beam of love-light move him right into your heart connection with the divine. Take three deep breaths now and allow Rodney to leave. Breathe... breathe... breathe...*"

"*Elizabeth, what are the main lessons for you from Rodney's lifetime?*"

"*Rodney found the courage to change the pattern of his life and it set him free to become his truest self. He showed me what is really important, namely to find my own authentic self and to express it. Through the example of Rodney's life, I can see that the gifts of the personality: intellect, talents, skills, knowledge... these things are ephemeral. Attaching my ego identity to such things is a recipe for suffering. The really important things in life have nothing whatsoever to do with the illusion that is this reality. These are the gifts of the soul. I am so thankful to Rodney for these lessons!*"

"*Elizabeth, are there any other places that you need to visit from this lifetime? Anything that remains unfinished?*"

"*Not during this lifetime, no. But I find myself attracted to another scene after the ending of this lifetime. Another scene between lives.*"

"*Good, well go there now and tell me what you are experiencing.*"

"I'm with my spirit guide, Michael, again and we are reviewing the life that has just ended - Rodney's life. Michael says:

'Rodney, what have you learnt during this lifetime?' *and Rodney responds,* 'I've learnt to find my authentic heart connection to my own higher self. I've discovered that this is far more important than the things that the personality believes to be important. Things such as intellect and power, money, possessions and achievements. From a place of feeling small and powerless, I found my heart connection and I found my authentic power.'

"Sarah, Isn't it amazing! Rodney no longer stutters and he's able to express himself so well!"

"Well, Elizabeth, he's no longer constrained by the limitations of his physical incarnation. How does Michael respond?"

'Yes, you did find your heart connection and authentic power, Rodney. This was very well done. With this life you are almost done with physical incarnation into separation, duality and forgetting. However, I would like to propose one more lifetime.

In this next lifetime, you won't be limited at all in terms of your intellect or abilities. In fact, you will be choosing a personality of considerably above-average ability in all endeavours that are valued by the society in which the personality will find itself. In addition, you won't be limited by opportunities to advance.

The challenge in this next lifetime will be to find your heart connection from a place of privilege and every possible advantage. To value your heart connection above all luxuries and above all ego-inducements.

In Rodney's lifetime you really had no choice but to find your authentic self, as there were no external ego-validations to confuse you and pull you off course. In your lifetime as David, you had all the abilities and advantages and you lost yourself. Now it's time to put it all together. To have all the ego inducements possible and to still choose to find your authentic heart connection.

This will also be the lifetime in which you will integrate the learnings of all your previous lifetimes. You will find your heart connection and your authentic self from a place of forgetting and you will close the loop on several outstanding issues from previous lives. At the end of this lifetime you will have the opportunity to move onto a whole new dimension of existence; a whole new series of adventures.'

'That sounds great and I'm really looking forward to the adventure of this lifetime and those beyond. Let's get going!'

"Elizabeth, you seem a lot calmer now than you did before our session started."

"Yes, I am. Somehow seeing Rodney's life made me realise that I don't need to fear the changes coming in my life. If I go to my heart and find my own truth, I will be led to my highest expression of self and all will be well. I don't have to know right now where I will be going; what direction my life will be moving in. My ego doesn't have to be in charge and doesn't have to tell me what to do. I just need to stay connected to my heart and accept the place I am currently in.

Accept the learning and the growth and the change and
remain open to being shown my path forward.

I'm find that I'm really looking forward to seeing what
next week's session will bring!"

I sat in silent contemplation amongst the tree roots
for a long time pondering the questions that arose in my mind
as a result of the stories the Green Lady had told of David,
Rodney, Jean-Philippe and Didu. Then I asked, "*But, I don't
understand why Peer seemed to have caused trouble for Didu
and Jean-Philippe and not for Rodney or David. Wasn't he still
associated with the spirit being during the latter two
lifetimes?"*

"*Well, Peer wasn't a problem for Rodney because
Rodney wasn't driven by his ego, but rather by his heart.
David had a rather weakly developed ego and so there was no
real possibility of feeding for Peer in either of these two
lifetimes. As a result of this lack of feeding, Peer was in a
considerably weakened state, which made it relatively easy for
Elizabeth to work with Sarah to release him.*

*Shall we continue with the story? Next I am going to
tell you about another lifetime that Elizabeth and Sarah
encountered during their sessions. A lifetime that was all
about trusting the knowing, intuition and other messages from
the indwelling spirit. It's one thing to make the heart
connection; it's quite another to find the courage to act upon
the messaging we receive from that heart connection. You
see, the heart is the portal through which we access our higher
self. In this separation reality we don't know that we are
immortal, unlimited creator beings. We believe ourselves to
be frail, mortal and weak. It takes a lot of courage to begin to*

see ourselves as we truly are - to awaken to the illusion within the game. This is what the next lifetime - a human woman called Ana - is all about."

CHAPTER 11:
WEAVING TOGETHER THE
THREADS (PART 4)

"*Ok, Elizabeth, could you please describe for me what you see.*"

"*I see a barren, desolate hilltop... and a ruin of an old temple. The place of the gathering of the spirits. Deathly stillness and brooding heat. A massive storm is brewing. Now, ominous, billowing purple clouds are racing across the hilltop... incandescent flashes of lightning illuminating the hillside in psychedelic colours. Intense guilt, fear... no... terror compels me to move.*

Now I'm flying at immense speed, devouring the miles, the landscape disappearing far below. But still it gains on me; my pursuer is relentless. The terror, the darkness, draws ever closer.

I glance over my shoulder and my heart pounds and my breath rasps in my throat. It is almost upon me! There will be no escape this time. And then, with a silent, deadly swoop, I am engulfed. My mouth opens in a final, voiceless scream of agony. And then I am no more. Merciful oblivion."

"*Just keep breathing, Elizabeth. Calm, deep breaths. You're safe. Nothing can harm you here. Breathe.*"

"*Elizabeth, where are you now?*"

"I... I don't know. I'm nowhere and I am nothing. Just drifting... floating..."

"Elizabeth, this memory has arisen for a reason. There is something you need to address here so that you can move on with your life. I want you to return to the place in this lifetime that will provide you with the answers you seek. Go to that place now. What do you see?"

"I see a small village. The houses are very primitive. Wattle and daub, I think, with grass-thatched roofs. I'm an old woman standing in the village square, surrounded by a group of people. I think that I have some kind of psychic ability. I'm telling the villagers about a terrible threat that I have seen in my visions. It is a threat that will annihilate our way of life. That will destroy our village and our people. The villagers are terrified. They look to me for guidance, as they always have in the past. But the truth is that I really don't know what we should do.

I have seen in my visions the invading hordes and I have informed the village elders. They have decided that the men should go out to meet the threat before it reaches our village. Just as I saw in my vision, the men are completely outnumbered and they are all, to a man, slaughtered. But at least they were spared seeing their wives and children murdered. Next, the invaders will attack the village, kill all the old men and boys and murder, or take captive, the women and girl children. In my visions I have always seen our annihilation only. I have never seen any glimmer of hope for an alternative outcome.

I have no way of knowing what to do about the threat. But I see the fear on the faces of my neighbours and friends and so I present them with a plan. Something, anything, we can do to address the threat. In my heart I know it to be futile; I know that the men folk are already dead but I hide that fact from the villagers. They spring into action and we implement the plan. My role is to enter the hilltop temple of the spirits, where I will attempt to assist the villagers' efforts by interceding with the spirits in a state of trance.

But, just as I had seen in all my visions, it is absolutely futile. In my trance state I watch from the hilltop temple as my friends and neighbours are all either killed or captured. My guilt and fear overwhelms me and my spirit flies away to try and escape. But that too is futile and the evil catches up with me.

The enemy discover my defenceless body in the temple and, with one thrust of a spear, I am killed. All my talents and abilities have come to naught. I was completely unable to do anything to save those whom I loved the most."

"Elizabeth, bring that wise woman that you were to your mind-space. Describe for me what you see."

"Ana is standing before me now. She is tiny and wiry; with a leathery, wrinkled face and intense, fiercely intelligent, but compassionate black eyes. She is dressed in a coarsely woven brown robe that covers her sparse, grizzled hair."

"Elizabeth, what would you like to say to Ana?"

"Ana, this was not your fault. During your lifetime you used your abilities to help the villagers and many benefited from your healing, knowledge and insight. There was no way you could have prevented this disaster from happening. You didn't have the power or the ability. It was going to happen, regardless. At least you gave the villagers a sense of purpose by providing them with a plan to try and save themselves. At least they didn't die feeling like completely helpless victims. There is always a purpose to suffering, and *each and every villager that died that day, yourself included, had contracted for this to happen."*

"Elizabeth, what decision did you take, as a result of this lifetime that has impacted upon your current life?"

"I decided not to trust my own inner-knowing and I decided not to speak my truth, but rather to keep silent. I was afraid that I would cause harm or suffering to others by saying what I knew to be true."

"And how has that decision impacted on your life as Elizabeth?"

"I have often chosen to disregard my own inner-knowing and have instead mostly followed the dictates of my ego-mind."

"How has that worked for you, Elizabeth?"

"In terms of the measures of the world? Actually very well! I have earned money and respect and recognition. I have a fantastic career that is on a steep upward trajectory and I have all the luxurious possessions I could possibly ever have wanted. I have travelled the world, eaten at the finest restaurants, I own a fine home in an upmarket suburb, I drive an expensive sports car... well, I guess I have it all really."

"So, what's the problem then? Why the panic attacks? Why have you sought psychological help?"

"Because... because deep down my life feels utterly trivial and meaningless to me. My fancy possessions are just stuff and they often feel like a heavy burden to me. It doesn't feel as if I'm contributing anything of value to the world. I work eighty-hour weeks, I have no personal life, and I'm exhausted and bored and completely tired of the whole merry-go-round. I want something more. But I don't know what that is...

No, that's not true. I do know. I want to find out who I really am and what that real me wants from life. I want to live my life in a way that's congruent with the person I am and not the person the world believes me to be. I think the panic attacks are my ego fearing that it is losing control of my life and fighting to regain its control. A different, more authentic part of myself is clamouring to finally be heard."

"Well done! That's very good, Elizabeth. Is there anything else?"

"Yes. I have chosen not to speak my truth about others as well. I often suppress knowings that I have because I'm afraid that I might cause harm to others. On several occasions I have realised, after the fact, that my inner-knowing was completely correct. Often I could have helped people, had I shared my knowing. But I have kept quiet out of fear. Fear of ridicule, fear of being wrong and fear of causing harm. But perhaps I have caused greater harm by not speaking my truth."

"What is your new decision then, Elizabeth?"

"I will trust my heart; my inner knowing. I will actively seek out the knowledge and insight offered by my own inner-being. And I will offer this knowing to others when my heart tells me that it is appropriate for me to do so."

"Very good. I want you to invite Ana into your heart now, Elizabeth. Integrate Ana and all the knowledge and experience that she brings to your life. Take three deep breaths and on each out-breath, release all the negative energy remaining from Ana's lifetime. Breathe... breathe... breathe..."

"OK, Elizabeth, is there anything remaining from Ana's lifetime?"

"No, just calm warmth, and bliss and love."

"OK, I'm going to return you to normal consciousness now."

"Elizabeth, we have done some very good work together. I feel that we are really close to finding and dealing with all the outstanding issues associated with your other lives; the issues that are holding you back in this lifetime. How do you feel about that?"

"I agree, Sarah. I'm really looking forward to our next session. I believe that it may just be the final one required to bring about complete healing for me!"

The Green Lady paused in her narrative and smiled at me. *"Peter, do you see that Elizabeth could not have progressed further in her life had she not addressed and integrated the lessons from her lifetime as Ana? Although she hadn't been aware of it at the time, the panic attacks marked a pivotal decision point in her life. She needed to choose to start trusting in the direction of her own heart, the urging of her indwelling spirit, to step into her own authentic power, to find her own inner-truth and to become truly herself. None of that would have been possible without addressing the prior lifetimes and the integration of the lessons contained therein."*

"Yes, I can see that, but I do have a question. What would have happened if Elizabeth had not chosen to seek help from Sarah? If she had simply decided to stay on the anti-depressants and get on with her life, as most people would have done? I mean, how many people would have gone along

with the crazy stories that emerged during her sessions with Sarah!

I guess what I'm actually asking is where free will comes into all of this? Was it pre-ordained that Elizabeth would go to see Sarah, or was it a complete fluke? How much was Elizabeth's choice and how much was she prompted by her indwelling spirit to follow the life plan that had been set up pre-incarnationally?"

"That is a really good question, Peter. And it demonstrates to me that your own thinking is rapidly evolving. What I can tell you is this: although the life plan is set up pre-incarnationally, the personality has complete free will as to whether they will follow it or not. Elizabeth didn't have to do any of the processing she ended up doing. She was presented with various prompts and with the opportunities to do so, but she wasn't compelled to follow any of them. She could have continued to live her life of ego-gratification and to continue along her career path. Although it would have been a hard path for her, it would have been possible for her to choose a life that seemed to drag on, devoid of meaning, with the burden of panic attacks hanging over her head, staved off only by using heavy doses of mind- and emotion numbing psychopharmaceuticals...

And, in that case, she would have been offered new opportunities after the end of that lifetime; opportunities that would have enabled her to reach the understandings and learnings that her soul wished for her to have. It might have required another lifetime or two to achieve that, though.

Although the learnings required by the higher self will always eventually be achieved, nothing is pre-ordained and the personality is always free to choose. Within bounds of course. The soul will not permit the personality to go so far as to completely derail its goals. But, for all that, there is a wide range of possibility open to the personality. That is what makes the game so interesting and exciting!"

"Could Elizabeth possibly have made other choices that would have ensured that she reached this point at an earlier stage in her life, then?"

"Quite likely, yes. But it's really not a race to the finishing line of spiritual enlightenment, Peter! It's all about the experience of finding and expressing the authentic self, or the higher self, within this place of not-knowing; this place of deep forgetting. And, ultimately, all beings will reach that point; whether it takes a thousand lifetimes or only ten. As time does not exist outside of this reality, it really doesn't matter whether a being chooses to take the quickest point from A to B or the scenic route!"

"OK, I think I understand. But I do have one small question that's puzzling me. I had thought that each lifetime took place at a later point in history. I mean, disregarding for a moment Sera's life, which I have no way of knowing when it occurred; Didu's story took place in an ancient civilisation, whereas Jean-Philippe's story mostly took place in the early nineteenth century. Then David's story was set in the early twentieth century and Rodney's story in the mid twentieth century, with Elizabeth's story taking place in the late twentieth century. But now Ana's story seems to have taken place at a much earlier time. What gives?"

"Peter, you disappoint me! Remember, I told you that the higher self is outside of time and that time is only a constraint experienced within this reality we currently inhabit? As such, the higher self can express itself into any time frame or dimension, or indeed on any planet, in order to have the experiences that it requires next on its journey. The Earth time *progression of the stories that you mentioned is purely coincidental. Of course certain time periods and each of the two genders do allow for specific experiences that are more difficult to obtain under other circumstances."*

"OK, sorry. You have emphasised that point to me several times. I guess it's just that I have encountered this notion about past-lives that each must follow the other in a time-bound sequentiality. Some people even believe that one must have an incarnation every so many years and during each era."

"Yes, I know that many hold onto these mistaken ideas. It's because it is so difficult for the time-bound human mind to come to grips with a non-linear progression of inter-connected lives."

"I can accept that. So, what's next in the story?"

"Well, Elizabeth still has a few outstanding issues from other lives to address. Then she can freely move into a place of unfettered expression of her authentic self."

"Can you describe to me what you are seeing, Elizabeth?"

"I am in a circle with twelve others. But... hang on... this is very weird because we aren't strictly speaking individuals, as humans are. We are different perspectives; different thought forms that have arisen from within someone's mind. No, wait, it's more than that. It seems as if this is all actually taking place within the mind of the One. Each thought form holds a perspective and together they form a council that has been created to make a very important decision. I can see that the strength of this community is in its unity. The individuals on their own have no real power and

they arise to fulfil a function for a short time before merging once more into the Unity. This is seriously strange! From which deep, dark recesses of my crazy mind did this story arise?!"

"Trust that there is a reason for this story to be surfacing right now, Elizabeth. There is something for you to learn here, just as there is in every single story that arises. Trust that. Tell me more about what you are experiencing."

"It is a time of a terrible threat to our Unity. There has been an attack from a race of beings, technologically far superior to the Unity. They have offered an ultimatum. It is the sacrifice of the few for the many. The deal offered is this: if the Council separates, gives up their Unity and allows the aggressors into the circle, the Unity will ultimately be protected. In addition, they have been promised that they will be given access to opportunities for expansion, the likes of which they have never before experienced. If they resist, the entire Unity will be destroyed. But there is a silent serpent in their midst.

In one of the thought-forms, Sera, the one with whom I am identified, individual thought, and hence the ability to act as an individual, has arisen. This is the first time that this has happened and, with it, individual ego has also arisen. Sera is able to screen its thoughts from the Unity for the first time and Sera has developed a sense of being special, of being more-than the others. Sera has made a deal with the technology beings that it will convince the Council to accept the proposal made by these beings. In return, Sera will be assured of its continued survival as an individual. It's a true Faustian bargain."

"What happens?"

"I guess, kind of inevitably, it is a trick. The Council allows the technology beings access, which leads directly to the destruction of the entire race. Their Unity was their strength and, had they maintained their Unity, they would have been impervious to their aggressors."

"And what happened to Sera?"

"Well, Sera was not destroyed. But was set adrift, alone, forever. Sera realised that in its Unity it had had all that it had needed. It desired its individuality and, in so doing, lost everything."

"What is the message of this lifetime for you, Elizabeth?"

"Acting from a place of ego leads to a far lower quality outcome than when one acts from a place of heart-centeredness. The ego leads us deeper into the illusion; deeper into the game. But the heart leads us out of the illusion of separation and back home to Oneness."

"That is a remarkable insight, Elizabeth. Bring the Council to your mind now. Describe to me what you see."

"Well, it's not seeing, as such, because these beings don't really have a physical form in the way that we would understand it. It's more of a sensing of a presence... A kind of a feeling and a knowing... This is really hard for me to describe!"

"What would you like to tell them?"

"I betrayed our Unity. I let the desires and the fears of my newly-emerged ego take precedence over the good of the One. I acted in what I thought were my own best interests and, in so doing, brought about the destruction of the One. I am deeply sorry."

"What is the response from the One, Elizabeth?"

"*Beloved one from the Oneness, do you not see that it is simply a matter of perspective? If you believe in the illusion of your separateness, then, yes, the Unity is destroyed. Then you find your actions - your betrayal of the Unity - to be unforgivable. However, if you believe in the truth that we are One, then there is nothing to be forgiven. The One can never be destroyed. It is always just a matter of perspective.*

There is always the choice to move ever deeper into the game; ever deeper into ego and individuality and separation. But then there is also another choice, which is to awaken to the illusion. It is only a game. It is all just a dream. All is One. All has always been One and will always be One. The destruction of the Unity was simply an illusion; simply a perspective.

Breathe in... breathe out... creation and destruction.... do and be... reality and illusion... choices, choices... choices and consequences... But all will eventually fall away and the one, objective truth will be revealed. All is ultimately One."

"*Elizabeth, what meaning and value does all of this hold for your current life?*"

"*Everything is a matter of perspective. And my life - the perspective I choose to hold - that too is my choice. And my choices create my reality. So, I guess I need to decide which reality I am going to choose to create for myself. Which reality do I choose to inhabit?*"

"*And how will you go about making these important choices, Elizabeth?*"

"*I will go to my heart to access the highest version of myself that I possibly can. I will be guided by my heart and not by my ego.*"

"Elizabeth, are you prepared to live with the consequences to your life and your career that such heart-guided choices might imply?"

"Yes, I am! I've tried living my life with my ego in the driver's seat and it's not making me happy. Despite having everything the world tells me that I should want, I'm still not truly happy. Now I'm going to try a different way. I'll make my own life an experiment in following my heart, wherever it may lead me. I will see if that choice will bring me greater joy."

The Green Lady paused for a long while in her narrative and we simply sat in silence as I digested all of the stories I had been told and wrestled with their implications. Eventually I looked up, directly into her startling, emerald-green eyes, and just shook my head, disbelieving.

"Wow! I don't actually know what to say. What incredible stories! But they all seem to point to the same lesson, namely the importance of trusting the heart above the ego. And, ironically, this seems to be what my own story is all about too!"

"Yes, Peter, you are exactly right. This is why you have been called to write this story. But don't make the mistake of demonising the ego as so many spiritual traditions do. The ego is not the enemy. Without ego, you would never get out of bed in the morning. Without ego, humankind would certainly never have accomplished any of the magnificent acts of creativity, such as great works of art, the wonders of science, space exploration, bringing new children into the world... even the writing of this book requires an immense effort of ego, Peter.

But, what is important to remember is that ego makes an excellent servant, but a terrible master. The leadership and direction should come from the heart, for the heart is the portal to the highest self and the way to access that divine spark within. Then the heart should give the ego the job of getting things done in the world.

This reality is a beautiful, magnificent illusion; an amazing game. But don't forget that it is only a game and that, like all games, it will eventually come to an end and you will return to your true nature, which is Oneness.

Attaching your ego to the outcomes of the game is a recipe for suffering. Enjoy the game, but always remain heart-connected; connected to the deepest truth of who and what you truly are. These are the lessons provided by the stories I have shared."

"But, where do we go when we are done with this reality?"

"Ah, that, my friend, is a story for another day! I'll see you next week, same place, same time."

And, with that, the Green Lady arose and silently glided into the forest, leaving me to ponder for a long time on all that I had been told.

Until my cramped legs and growling stomach alerted me to the fact that it was almost sunset and that I had a long hike and an even longer drive down the mountain before I could satisfy my hunger. I left the clearing in the forest, utterly bemused by the way the story had turned out, but also eagerly anticipating the following week.

Chapter 12:
All is Finally Revealed

I could scarcely contain my impatience to get answers to several questions that had been troubling me during the past week. The Green Lady had barely sat down on her log the following week before I burst out with the first of my concerns. "*I have some questions for you. There are a few things that have been bothering me since we last spoke. Firstly, what happened to Elizabeth? She underwent such a massive change of heart and mind during her sessions with her hypnotherapist that I'm sure her life changed quite dramatically afterwards. Could you finish telling me the story of Elizabeth, please?*"

"*Of course, I'd love to! Elizabeth did indeed experience a radical transformation during her sessions with her hypnotherapist. Elizabeth's life is what we call an integrative lifetime or an ascension lifetime. She needed to integrate all of the outstanding lessons of a number of different lifetimes into her current life. In addition, she needed to address any outstanding karmic issues with other beings that she had encountered in other lifetimes. Most of all, she needed to raise her consciousness to the levels required to finally leave this game of separation so that she could begin to engage in new games at a whole other level of consciousness.*"

"So, what... did Elizabeth ascend up into the clouds or something?"

"No, my friend, we're not talking about ascension of the physical body, but rather ascension of consciousness. It's all about awakening to the truth within the illusion, within the game. It's about becoming aware that you are not only this limited personality that you believe yourself to be, but also a powerful, immortal creator being.

In practical terms, Elizabeth eventually abandoned her career and her busy, materialistic city life and she went to live a very simple existence in the forests of this area. Within a few years of moving to the forest, she met, and married, a wonderful man called Bill. He was an artist and a free spirit and the person that Elizabeth had been whilst living in the city and pursuing her corporate career would never even have noticed someone like Bill. Or she would probably have dismissed him out of hand as a potential partner because he lacked drive and ambition and was not successful in the ways in which she had previously valued. But Bill was a deeply spiritual, caring and heart-centred person and together they were able to support and encourage each others' spiritual growth and learning. It was to be a partnership that would last for over thirty years.

Elizabeth lived out her natural life in her forest home, gradually learning to access ever higher and higher versions of her most authentic self. She learned to trust her own truth and to be guided by her own inner-knowing.

This inner-wisdom led Elizabeth to becoming involved in various conservation activities in the forests and natural surroundings of her home. She wrote several books and articles on the topic of conservation and she applied her intellect and organisational skills to many initiatives that had a very positive effect on protecting the forests she grew to love. She also learned to grow organic vegetables and played a large role in training disadvantaged young people to grow their own food and thereby become more self-sufficient.

According to the standards of the world, Elizabeth abandoned her lucrative and promising career in order to live a rather small and marginal life in a remote and isolated place in the forests of her country. But, according to the inner-truth of Elizabeth's heart, her life became ever richer and more meaningful and fulfilling. She grew to love, and formed a very deep connection with, the forests in which she lived. This connection was to play a pivotal role in her next adventure."

"Oh really? I'd love to hear about that. But first, there's something I've always wondered about. What's the deal with karma? You previously mentioned that Elizabeth had to address various outstanding issues with respect to other lives. Could we collectively refer to those issues as karma?"

"Karma is often misunderstood. Some humans think that if you've been "bad" in one lifetime then you'll receive your come-uppance in another lifetime. But it's not like that at all. It's really more helpful to think of it as a process of balancing. So, if in one lifetime, you have contracted to play the role of perpetrator to another being's role of victim, then you and that being might decide to balance that out by reversing the roles in another lifetime. It's never about punishment for wrongdoing. On the level of the spirit being, things are perceived very differently than when you are experiencing the limited expression of a single lifetime."

"You've spoken about contracts before. Does that mean that we agree with another being that we will be

victimised by them in a lifetime? Why would we do that? It doesn't make sense to me!"

"And, it wouldn't because you are viewing this from your limited human perspective, which is all that you have right now. But beings can, and often do, contract with each other pre-incarnationally to play out certain roles in a lifetime. These roles allow them to have various experiences, which, in turn, allow them to discover things about themselves and to learn and grow. Remember Rodney? Well, pre-incarnationally he contracted with the higher selves of the boys who were to bully him so that they could all learn through this interaction. As you could see from the story of Rodney, there was indeed much that he learnt from this interaction, which led, ultimately, to the elevation of his consciousness.

You see, Peter, in order to play the victim game, a perpetrator is required. And there can be no perpetrator without a victim. In fact, there is an additional role in this game as well - that of the rescuer. Each of these roles requires the other two roles in order to function. There can be no rescuer without the victim who needs to be rescued and the perpetrator who causes the victim to require rescuing! And so on. This victim-perpetrator-rescuer drama is played out, over-and-over again in this reality. It allows for wonderful growth and learning about the nature of the self.

These roles can last for a short while during a life, or indeed for an entire lifetime. Sometimes even for several lifetimes. And we move from one role to the next, learning about ourselves in the process. But, whether we play the role of victim or perpetrator or rescuer, it's all just part of the same game - the victim game. And it's a game which keeps us firmly stuck in this duality reality.

The only way to get out of this victim game is to finally realise that we are not victims, rescuers or perpetrators, but creator-beings. We are creators who have created for ourselves the illusion of being limited victims."

"Does this mean that Rodney then bullied those same boys in another lifetime?"

"The answer to that question is a matter of perspective. The soul that identifies itself as Rodney and the souls that identify themselves as his perpetrators may, in fact, agree to have a direct reversal. But when you understand that there is only really the One acting upon itself, then you realise that every other being is the other-self. We are always partnering in every contract with an aspect of the One. Which, ultimately, is ourself.

As Rodney, the self was bullied by the other. As Jean-Philippe, the other was abused and vitimised by the self. It is not possible to state categorically whether these two others are the same other. It is all simply a matter of perspective.

There is another very important reason for playing various different roles: it allows us to finally begin to relinquish our judgements of others when we reach our ascension lifetime. When I can finally understand that anything that anyone else has done, I too, under certain circumstances, am capable of doing, then that allows me to begin to find love and acceptance of myself and love and acceptance of the other. As we will see later, this is the way in which we finally ascend out of the system.

Peter, we will discuss this all in further detail a little later on. But, for now, I think it's time for our final story. Actually it's a continuation of the life story of Elizabeth, only several years later. Then I will take up the story in the spirit realm, directly after Elizabeth's life ended. This is the story that immediately precedes the emergence of the Green Lady!"

"Oh, at last! Well, please tell me. I can't wait to hear this one! I'll save the rest of my questions for later."

I settled back against the tree trunk, pen and paper at the ready.

The final day of Elizabeth's life began like any other day. She awoke at dawn and did the yoga stretches she had been doing every single morning for the past forty years. She could still complete her stretching routine, even though it now took double as long to do as it had in her younger days. She was still slender, her back straight and upright, despite being in her mid-eighties. Although recently she had been troubled by a touch of arthritis in her hands, and her hipbones sometimes ached in the mornings or if the weather was cold.

Since her beloved husband had passed away five years earlier she had been increasingly lonely and isolated and she often went for weeks without speaking to a single other soul. She hadn't written anything for quite some time now and she had gradually relinquished all the conservation activities that had kept her so busy during her younger years. Her increasing isolation didn't trouble her overly much as she continued having conversations with her husband, Bill, even though he was no longer there in the flesh. At least he no longer interrupted her and she was always able to have the last word!

"Bill, I'm thinking of having strawberries for breakfast. The first spring berries should be ripe by now. What say you we go and pick them?"

Elizabeth grabbed her wicker basket and carefully made her way down the kitchen stairs to the back garden, clutching tightly to the banister, as she was a little unsteady on her feet this particular morning. She smiled to see the bright-red berries glistening with dew in the early morning sun. *"You see, Bill. I told you they'd be ripe, didn't I? Strawberries and yoghurt for breakfast. That'll keep you nice and regular, my boy!"*

But, as Elizabeth bent down to pick the first strawberry, she suddenly felt dizzy and un-coordinated and the red berries and green leaves blurred together before her eyes. She listed to one side and then fell, as her left leg suddenly refused to support her weight any longer and gave way beneath her. Elizabeth crumpled onto the ground, her head coming to rest on the damp strawberry leaves. She lay there quite calmly, inhaling the scents of moist earth, green leaves and the sweet tang of crushed berries, the sun gently warming the side of her face. *"Ah, Bill, so this is how it all ends. How interesting! Well, not so bad, all things considered. At least I didn't leave the stove on! I'll just lay here and rest a bit until you come to fetch me, shall I?"* she whispered beneath her breath.

And, with that thought, a red fog clouded Elizabeth's mind, and by-and-by her heart pumped its final beat and she exhaled her final breath. All was very quiet for a long, long moment. And then Elizabeth heard a soft voice calling her, *"Liza, Liza, come my little one, it's time to go now!"* Elizabeth opened her eyes and there was Gran, whom she hadn't seen for over sixty years.

"Granny, you've come for me! But, where's Bill? Don't tell me he's late again! That man has the very worst

sense of timing! Or did he perhaps get the wrong day? Oh wait, I forgot! You never met Bill, did you?"

"I actually have met your Bill, my love. He's a wonderful man and so very witty too! You'll see him shortly, Liza-love. And your mother and father, and, indeed, your birth mother too. But come now, we've got to go. Your journey in this place is finally over. There are so many interesting things we have to do and so many fascinating new places we can visit."

Elizabeth and her Gran left hand-in-hand and we will draw a veil on the experiences that she had for the next while. We rejoin Elizabeth and Michael, her guide, in the place of reviewing.

I sat for a moment pondering the story of Elizabeth's final day on Earth. Then something occurred to me.

"I've just realised that if Elizabeth was born in the 1970's, she must now be around my own age. And yet, I have just heard the story of her final day! How weird and troubling it is to me to try and get my head around this issue of time. I also realise that it's entirely possible that I might even encounter Elizabeth here in Knysna, seeing as she also lives in the area! But wait! Won't this be a problem for her? I mean... what if she was to read my book and recognise her story and then discover what she will do with her life and how she will die? Won't she be upset with me for telling her story without her approval? And doesn't this seem to indicate that there really is no free will after all? Oh no, I'm totally confused now!"

"Peter, there are no mistakes. If it is the soul purpose of both Elizabeth and yourself that you should meet, then of course you will meet. And if it is the purpose of Elizabeth's soul that she should read your book, then that is exactly what will happen. And you will each provide the other with exactly the input that you have contracted to provide._

But, from the perspective of the personality, you definitely do have free will. You can decide for yourself exactly what you will do next, as can Elizabeth. You can each of you decide to follow the guidance of your indwelling spirit, via your heart connection, or to disregard it entirely. And each will experience the consequences of those choices.

Be still now Peter. Close your eyes and feel your physical heart beating. Feel for your heart connection. What does it tell you to do?"

I sat for a long while, feeling my heart beat slowing down, as a sense of certainty gradually dawned upon me.

"_I must write and publish this book. That is all I know for sure, for now._"

The Green Lady slowly nodded her head at me and then said, "_If that is what your heart is telling you to do, then that is what you must do. Always trust the guidance of your heart. Your heart offers you the quickest and most painless route through the confusion that is physical life in this reality. Stay in this moment of knowing and don't borrow trouble and worries from the future. Trust that all is proceeding perfectly according to the plans of your higher self._

In fact, Peter, as you begin to move along your ascension path, you will start to find that all ideas of conventional morality, right and wrong, good and evil, should and shouldn't... these ideas gradually begin to fall away. Such ideas are all irrevocably bound to this system of duality. Gradually the only concern becomes to follow the direction offered by your higher self, which is directly accessed via the *portal of your heart. And, as you are able to increasingly access this inner wisdom of your most God-like self, you begin to increasingly access that perspective until you finally awaken to the knowing that you <u>are</u> actually your higher self expressing itself into this place of forgetting. You awaken to the reality within the dream. This is what many mystics have termed, enlightenment.*

At that point you are pretty much done with the game of incarnation and will move onto other adventures in which you will create in full knowledge of who you truly are. You will be done with the victim game for good. But it all starts with the decision to keep returning to your heart's knowing for direction and guidance."

The Green Lady and I sat quietly for a while, just being in the moment, as I allowed myself to relinquish all of my concerns and to simply feel my heart connection. It was incredibly peaceful. How very different our lives would be if we were able to find, and always live within, this moment of now, instead of fretting about the past and the future, I mused.

"Yes, indeed, Peter, that would certainly reduce your pain and suffering to an absolute minimum," the Green Lady said, reading my thoughts with ease. *"Your so-called memories are simply stories that you tell yourself about the life that lies behind you, about the world and about other people and events that you have experienced. But there are always other ways in which you could interpret the events of your past; additional information that you failed to absorb as it didn't fit in with your thoughts about yourself at the time. And this information could completely change the memories, and therefore, the stories that you tell yourself about your life. But you attach your sense of identity to these very limited*

stories, which causes you great pain and suffering. Equally, your fears about the future are simply stories that you tell yourself in order to try and deal with your fears and insecurities. Instead of helping, these stories actually cause you even more pain and suffering.

But if you were able to remain centred in the present moment, you would only have to deal with what this moment brings you. You would be able to extract so much more value from the moment without the burden of your thoughts and fears about the past and the future. It's something to strive towards, isn't it?

But now, if you are ready, perhaps we can continue with the story of Elizabeth? Elizabeth is in the place of the reviewing of her life that has just concluded..."

"Well, Elizabeth, here we are! You've come to the end of this particular game. How do you feel about it all?"

"It's been an incredible ride! Such highs and lows. Such beauty and sadness; such joy and pain. But now that I get to the end of this cycle of lifetimes, I can say, unequivocally: it was <u>so</u> worth it. By forgetting who I truly am and by descending into that place of separation; that place of deep forgetting, I have been able to really discover myself from a place of not-knowing. I have been able to truly see myself in the mirror of the other; in the mirror of the world. I have learnt what it is that I will create when I have completely forgotten who I am. I have a whole new understanding of who and what I truly am now. I feel like I'm really done with the not-knowing part and I would really prefer not to do that again! I must say, I believe that I'm finally ready to move on

now; to start a whole new adventure at a whole new level of consciousness."

Michael nodded his head and smiled at Elizabeth, *"You have indeed learnt many things about yourself and you have contributed many valuable experiences and learnings to the consciousness of this separation reality, Elizabeth. But, before we move on, let's just do a final review of what you have learnt on this particular journey, through this particular series of lives.*

As you well know, the dimension in which the lives that we are currently reviewing took place is all about separation from your most God-like self and about deep forgetting. It is also a polarity reality, and the most obvious polarity is the split into the masculine and the feminine archetypes. However, there are many other polarities in this system. In fact, the system is all about you (and yours) versus me (and mine). There are polarities such as perceived right and wrong; good and evil; black and white, Christian and Muslim, God-fearing and atheist, youth and age, and many, many, many others. This system is about experiencing the self as separate, individual and different from the other, which leads directly to the experience of fear-induced loneliness and isolation. The greatest polarity of all, of course, is the separation that all those who journey there feel to be between themselves and the divine. This greatest polarity is called duality. The duality of God and self.

This is why it is so that the only way to move out of this system is to begin to love the self so magnificently that you are able to see God in the self, which directly leads to the ability to see God in all others. This resolves the duality consciousness back into unity consciousness. Since, with this awareness, you begin to see the same Great Spirit within yourself as is within all others. You then begin to see all others as simply other-selves. And so, very gradually, the loneliness and isolation begin to lift. Eventually, all the lost parts of self, and all the other selves must be integrated in order to move out of the system. Male and female, black and white, different religions, cultures, and belief-systems are eventually seen to be the same, and all eventually become One, as the system disintegrates and higher levels of consciousness are achieved.

But, obviously, before there can be an ascension out of this system, there is first the moving into the system to fully experience it. For you, this started with the lifetime as Sera. In that lifetime there was the very first arising of the individual self; of the individual ego. From out of the Unity, individuality arose. Inevitably, there was also the first encounter with the Other, in the form of the technology beings. This Other was seen to be different from self; negative and aggressive and threatening to the self, which led to fear. Fear will always lead to isolation and aloneness. In the lifetime as Sera, the desires of the individual ego resulted in separation from the Unity. In fact, the being called Sera believed that the destruction of the Unity had occurred as a result of its actions and, for the first time, alone-ness and loneliness was experienced.

Then, in the lifetime as Didu, we saw very clearly the contrast between the extreme masculine and extreme feminine archetypes, in both their positive and negative aspects, as typified by the Atlantean and Lemurian civilisations. Within Didu herself, we saw how the duality of conflicting masculine and feminine energies caused her considerable stress and pain. We also very definitely saw how this duality leads to separation and, eventually, to fear-induced isolation. Didu experienced herself as being isolated, alone and very much motivated by fear as a child slave ripped away from her home and family. In Didu's story we see yet again how destructive it can be when the ego is in control and the personality is driven by fear. Didu became a stranger to herself and to her people. As a result, she caused much pain and harm to herself and to many others. There were wonderful opportunities during this lifetime to experience the roles of both victim in the early life and perpetrator, later on during this lifetime.

In the lifetime of Jean-Philippe, we see again a lifetime of ego in the driver's seat. Just like most beings, he was actually looking for love, but he didn't know how to find authentic love and connection. And so Jean-Philippe sought instead a substitute for love, namely fear and respect and recognition, which he forced from others, using his physical strength and his many talents and advantages. What Jean-Philippe didn't realise was that the only love he really needed to find was love for himself, from within himself. He never was going to find what he needed and wanted outside of himself. This was certainly a lifetime of experiencing a very powerful ego, allowed to run rampant and we clearly saw the consequences of that. A lifetime as a rather extreme perpetrator of much harm to others.

David didn't allow his ego to run the show, but he was ineffective until he placed his sense of okay-ness in another. He never found his own heart-connection or his own sense of self and was extremely self-destructive as a result.

In the case of Rodney, we see a life of diminished physical and intellectual ability, which ultimately led to a discovery of the heart connection; a discovery of the authentic self. Rodney wasn't able to compete with anyone using his ego-mind or his physical strength. He had to find his own sense of self within, as he certainly wasn't going to be getting any significant recognition and affirmation from the outside world. Rodney's life is a perfect example of how, what seems to the personality, to the ego-mind, as a less successful lifetime, is actually a powerful opportunity to discover the authentic self. In Rodney's life, there was again a powerful victim experience and also the opportunity to experience playing the role of rescuer for the first time.

Ana's life was a powerful rescuer experience. Here was someone who had discovered her many authentic talents and gifts, and had developed these gifts of the higher self to the benefit of her community. Although again, from the perspective of the ego-mind, this lifetime did not end happily, it was still a very successful lifetime. Even though Ana's gifts did not enable her to save her people, or indeed herself, the lesson we learn is not to focus on the outcome of expressing the gifts. The reward is in finding, and expressing the authentic self; not in the outcome thereof. Focus on outcomes is a very human trait. The ego wants to have the gratification of achieving something tangible, which it finds to be useful and valuable and then the ego wants to attach itself to that perspective of itself. This will always, ultimately, lead to pain and suffering.

However, for the indwelling spirit, it's all about the process of discovery and expression of the self. This is the lasting outcome from a lifetime; the ego-achievements all amount to nothing once the personality dies.

Elizabeth, the integrative lifetime, brought together lessons from all the other lifetimes. She explored the ego-driven way of being in the corporate world, but then found her heart connection and chose differently. Elizabeth briefly explored being a victim to her panic attacks, but then chose to find healing; eventually coming to see herself as a creator being. She was also able to address several outstanding karmic issues from other lifetimes and to find healing for, and integration of, all the lost parts of herself. In addition, Elizabeth was able to close off the open contract with Peer.

In Elizabeth's later life, once she had moved to the forest, she began to find herself able to see God, not only within her own being, but also in the being of all others she encountered. When a being is able to see that every other it encounters is simply another self; when a being is able to love every other, no matter how different that other may appear from the outside, as another self, then that being is well advanced on their ascension path. And this is the path that leads out of duality and separation and forgetting. The path that leads directly back to Oneness. And this is the path that you are now firmly on, Elizabeth. You will have many more adventures as you progress on this path, but you will never again forget that you truly are a perfect expression of Divine Love.

And so now, Elizabeth, let's talk about what next lies ahead for you. From here on out there will be no more forgetting who and what you truly are. All future growth will be in full knowledge of your most Godlike self. In a way, though, this allows for less free will, which is exactly why separation and duality are so very useful for the evolution of a soul.

Elizabeth, you now certainly have the choice to move on to the next dimension of being.

Or... you have another choice, should you want it. A whole grand new adventure in consciousness, as it were!"

"Another choice? What would that be?"

"Well, Elizabeth, during this lifetime you have formed a very deep soul connection with the consciousness of the

forest. *You have begun to identify yourself with the forest and you have contributed your love and energy and intent toward helping and healing the forest and the surrounding areas. Isn't that so?"*

"Yes indeed. I have come to love the consciousness of the forest. It is magnificent and beautiful and it has inspired me and assisted me in the raising of my own consciousness and in the healing of my pain."

"Well, Elizabeth, you now have the opportunity to return once again to the reality you have just left. But to return re-incarnated as the guardian of the forest itself. You will return with full knowledge of your own indwelling spirit - your own higher self - never to forget again. If this is your choice, then you will be contributing your energy and your spirit to the forest and, in so doing, to be a part of assisting the planetary consciousness also to ascend to the next dimension.

Each individual element of the forest has its own consciousness. Each plant and animal, every micro-organism, the air, the water, the soil... But the overall organising principle would be provided by your own consciousness. You would provide the higher-dimensional consciousness of the forest as a whole.

Think of it this way: a bee hive is the organising principle, or the overall consciousness, whereas the individual bees each have their own small consciousness. You would assist each of the individual consciousnesses in the forest to evolve; to ascend. And, in so doing, you would eventually ascend the overall consciousness of the forest to the next level. And, due to the interconnectedness of all things, you will assist the whole planet's nature-spirits to evolve. How do you feel about taking on that job for a while?"

"Well! What a surprise! But, of course, I always knew that the forest is a conscious, sentient being, albeit of a different kind to humans. Whenever I spent any length of time in the forest I would become aware of the presence of this being and I would try to communicate with this being by opening my heart and finding the connection within.

You know what? I would actually love to assist the forest in achieving its own ascension! I would love to be the spirit of the forest for as long as is required."

"Well, so be it then. You will provide the indwelling spirit for forest, wherever it might be found. Not just on the planet and in the dimension in which you lived out your last incarnation as Elizabeth, but also in many other dimensions and other planets of this reality where a similar expression occurs."

"How would this all work?"

"As we operate outside of time in spirit-space, you will obviously return to that reality at the very beginning of the evolution of the forest; at the very start of the development of the first micro-organisms and then the first proto-plants on each and every single planet and dimension and time-continuum where forest will eventually emerge. You will imbue the developing entity with your consciousness and assist it in gaining ever greater and greater self-awareness until the point at which it will achieve sufficient consciousness to ascend from that reality to the next.

You will also, as the spirit of the forest, engage with many other sentient beings, including humans and other beings on many other planets in many other systems. Here, your experiences of your several lifetimes will assist you in understanding these beings and in helping them to begin elevating their own consciousness too."

"How amazing! And who would have thought that when I was Elizabeth, feeling such a deep connection with the spirit of the forest, that I was actually connecting with myself, as the indwelling consciousness! What a beautifully intricate dance of inter-connecting lifetimes, all coming together to create patterns of wonderful meaning. Each life truly is just like a jewel reflecting every other life and being reflected by every other life in turn."

"This is the message of ascension, Elizabeth. That every other life you encounter is actually you*. There is only One of us here, experiencing itself as many, for the purpose of discovering who and what it truly is. As you say, an exquisitely intricate dance of forgetting and remembering, of expressing and re-integrating, of breathing in-and-out, of be-ing and do-ing.*

And so begins your next adventure..."

"Oh. My. God! So you truly were Elizabeth and Sera and Didu and Jean-Philippe and all the others too. These have truly been your own, other lifetime, stories that you have been sharing!"

"Yes Peter. All of those lives are different aspects of me and they tell the story of how I have become the Green Lady, the indwelling spirit of the forest."

"But, how long have you been the Green Lady for?"

"Since the very first proto-bacteria emerged four billion years ago on Earth, I have been present, witnessing the progression to ever higher forms of life, lending my energy and my intent to drive the process forward."

"Four billion... Oh my God, you're ancient!"

"*Not a very flattering thing to say to a lady, I dare say!*"

"*I'm sorry, but the mind simply boggles! And when will your job finally end?*"

"*While there are still trees on Earth and on the other planets and other dimensions at this level of consciousness, I will continue to do my job of protecting and nurturing the forest. And when the final tree has disappeared and the spirit of the forest reaches the next level of consciousness, then I will move on.*"

"*What? Wait a minute! What do you mean, 'other planets'? Does that mean that there are other planets similar to this one on which there are forests?*"

"*Of course! Were you not paying attention while I was telling the story? Did you really think that this was the only planet upon which forest has evolved? Many of these forests are at different times or in different dimensions, but there are literally millions of places in which the spirit of forest is expressed. And wherever there is forest... there I am.*"

"*But you seem to have become quite involved in the lives of certain human beings in this reality?*"

"*Well, because I too have had several lives as a human being, I can identify with the fears and hopes and challenges of being human. As the spirit of the forest I can also play a role in teaching and guiding individual humans in their own evolution. It is my greatest joy to do this work. This is partly why I have decided to tell you my story. It is also why I have engaged with authors and poets and thinkers and dreamers and eco-warriors and many other so-called eccentrics over the years. To bring attention to the plight of the forests. To make human beings aware of the important role the forests have to play as the lungs of the planet. But,*" *even more importantly, the role the forests play in fostering the evolution of consciousness.*

 Similarly, my lifetimes on other planets and in other dimensions, most of which I haven't even told you about, have prepared me to engage with those life forms present there and assist where I can in the evolution of consciousness."

 "Oh, so there have been other lives that you haven't told me about?"

 "Of course! Each of us has many, many lives. I have simply told you about the handful of lives that Elizabeth still needed to heal and integrate before she could ascend her consciousness out of duality. But there were many other lifetimes; in fact, series of lifetimes, in which different lessons were learned; in which different aspects of self were explored."

 "Wow! I never realised what an important and influential being I was interacting with! I am honoured that you have included me in your plans. I really do hope that my books will make a difference to your cause."

 "Peter, no one being is more important than any other. You are seeing me from the very limited perspective of this time-bound life of yours as a human male on planet Earth. I can guarantee you that, were you able to now clearly see your own higher self, you would be awestruck by who and what you truly are when you are not forgetting who and what that is!

 As for your books; they <u>will</u> make a difference, Peter. But please remember; it's not the ego gratifications of book sales and favourable reviews that are important. What is important is that you find and express your most authentic self through your writing and through everything else that your heart calls you to do. When you do that, you make the biggest possible difference: the difference to yourself. Which makes, *of course, a difference to the One, because, always remember, there is only One of us here!*

And now, our time together has come to an end. I have told you my story. Now it's up to you to tell this story to the world. It's been a real pleasure engaging with you, my friend."

"Wait! Don't go yet! I have so many more questions for you."

"Peter, you don't need me to answer your questions anymore. You can find all the answers you seek within yourself. Simply walk in the forest and allow the spirit of the place to calm your mind. Allow yourself to reside in a place of love and gratitude. Then reach within and you will always find exactly what you need. Goodbye, Peter."

And, with that, the Green Lady turned and left the clearing for the final time. I had a very powerful inner-knowing that I wouldn't be seeing her in that form ever again in this lifetime and a part of me felt utterly bereft. She had had such an incredibly powerful, positive influence on my life and our weekly meetings in the forest clearing had been the highlight of my week.

But another part of me knew that her teachings and guidance had changed my life forever. She had, for a brief moment, played the role of rescuer to my victim, but it was now time for both of us to relinquish these roles. I needed to find my own creator-nature, which I now was certain that I would. I was, thanks to the wonderful intervention of the Green Lady, stepping out onto a whole new path, which would lead me to ever more authentic expressions of self. It was a path that would allow me to elevate my own consciousness and eventually lead me to my own ascension out of this system.

But that is a story for another day...

Thank you for reading my book. I really loved writing it! If you enjoyed it, won't you please take a moment to leave me a review at your favourite online retailer?
- *Lisa Picard*

Discover other titles by Lisa Picard, including **The Green Lady** (book 1 of this series), available as both an e-book and as a paperback at your favourite online retailer.

MEET THE AUTHOR

I am an ex-corporate warrior who, like so many of the characters in **The Green Lady, Books I and II** had a transformative experience in the forests of Knysna several years ago. I recorded a diary of my experience, including my mystical moment and the process of moving to the forests and constructing my own home, with my partner, Arn. You are invited to read all about it on my website[2].

2   http://thegreenlady.zingdad.com/about/diary-from-ego-to-heart.html

his life-altering experience was the catalyst that eventually led to my leaving my city life and corporate job and moving to a remote smallholding in the Outeniqua Mountains of South Africa's Garden Route.   My life partner, fellow author and spiritual healer, Arn Allingham, and I built our off-the-grid home with our own hands. As of 2010, we have been enjoying a simple, but deeply connected, life here on the border of the beautiful indigenous forest.   It is my greatest joy and the expression of my most authentic self to share my love and appreciation of the forests with others through my writing.

Connect with me:
Visit my website at thegreenlady.zingdad.com
Follow my blog thegreenlady.zingdad.com/blog
Visit my Facebook page at facebook.com/thegreenladybook

You can read on my website about my personal journey from ego to heart in the diary that I wrote documenting my transition from my city life to the life that I currently lead.

Additional writings, including a few short stories, can also be found on my website.

Many of the themes in **The Green Lady, Books I and II** are explored at far greater depth in the book, **The Ascension Papers**, written by my life partner, Arn (Zingdad) Allingham. This transformative and deeply healing e-book is available for free from his website[3]. Should you prefer a paperback book, then you can also order one off Arn's website.

---

3   zingdad.com

Besides being an author, Arn is also a talented healer and past-life re-integration facilitator. Just as the character Elizabeth in this book found the healing for her soul that allowed her to blossom eventually into the Green Lady, so too might it be your path to heal and re-integrate your past lives and, in so doing, discover your own magnificent soul's purpose. If you know this to be so - or would like to explore this possibility with a gifted healer - then I invite you to visit Arn's website to find out more about his **Soul Re-integration**[4] healing modality. He also offers some truly life-changing materials such as the "**Create Yourself, Create Your Life**" workbook and the "**Dreamer Awake!**" multimedia seminar series.

Should you be interested in combining a visit to the magnificent Knysna forests with powerful spiritual healing, then check out Arn's **African Spiritual Safaris** on his website.

You too may possibly meet the Green Lady for yourself!

---

4   Again, you can find all of these offerings at zingdad.com

Q&A with the Author

Are The Green Lady books written for adults or for children?
Book I was written for children of all ages who sense and appreciate the deep mystery and wonder of the forests. **Book I** can definitely be enjoyed by teenagers and, obviously, by adults. **Book II**, due to its more complex and perhaps darker, more mature themes, is for adults.

What was your inspiration for The Green Lady books?
The magnificent beauty of the forests of South Africa's Garden Route, but also forests that I have visited all over the world, inspired the writing of both books. There is some incredible connection, a sense of peace and indescribable elation, that I feel whenever I am in the forest. In addition, my own personal spiritual journey provided inspiration and material for the writing of **Book II**.

It is often said that all novels are autobiographical. Is this the case for The Green Lady books?
Both books are set in the Garden Route of South Africa, and mostly in the town of Knysna, which is the closest town to where I live. So, many of the places I mention in the book are real. However, the characters and events are all purely fictional, although, like most authors, I am often inspired by people I have met or experiences I have had.

I have included several of the themes of my own life and personal development during the past five years or so in **The Green Lady, Book I**. Such themes include: connecting with the heart, trusting your own inner guidance and the search for meaning and purpose in life. Also, many of the characters in **Book I** represent different aspects of my own personality and of my passions. For example, the passion of Benjamin Leigh in the story, **Expression of Your Authentic Self**, for alien vegetation management is also a reflection of one of my own passions. The story of Greg and Sandi in **Follow Your Heart** reflects a part of the journey of my partner and myself in building our own off-the-grid home, even though we did use a more conventional building method than the characters chose to use. The peak experience of Ken in the story of the same name and also of a few of the other characters is based upon such an experience that I personally had, which ultimately led to my own move to Knysna.

The Green Lady, Book II takes readers on an adventure that spans many different times and worlds, but the underlying spiritual themes are inspired by my own journey over the past few years.

So, yes, I suppose that both books are, to some extent, autobiographical in nature.

Have you ever met the Green Lady yourself?
I think that a part of me IS actually the Green Lady! When I am in the forest and experiencing that connection I mentioned before, I am often convinced that I am being observed by some greater entity. It often feels to me as if the forest is communicating with me on a very deep level and I draw such energy and inspiration from the place that... how can there not be a Green Lady!

Like many of the characters in the book, you too have moved from the city to the small town of Knysna. Tell your readers a bit about your journey.

I was a boardroom warrior in a large, multinational corporate when I had a transformative experience in the Knysna area. You can read more about my experience in my diary that is available on my website[5]. My life partner and I, like several of the characters in my stories in **The Green Lady, Books I and II**, liquidated our assets and moved to a small community, high up in the Outeniqua Mountains and bordering on the indigenous forest, where we built, mostly with our own hands, an off-the-grid home. This is where we still live and where I continue to write.

What is so special about Knysna and the surrounding forests?

It is a magical, exquisitely beautiful place. I've travelled extensively all over the world but this place remains my home and the only place I want to be. Come for a visit and see for yourself!

Will there be further Green Lady books?

That will depend on whether my lovely green muse decides to tap me on the shoulder once more to gain my attention! For now, my next book will be exploring the theme of embracing the inner-feminine; and, specifically, the inner-crone. I will again be using fairy tale archetypes to gradually guide the reader to a deeper understanding of complex spiritual themes. Look out for my next book in 2016!

Why did you decide to write a book?

---

5   http://thegreenlady.zingdad.com/about/diary-from-ego-to-heart.html

I've always written, as a way of working things out in my own mind, as an expression of my inner-self or just for fun. But **The Green Lady** books asked me to write them and so I had to oblige.

You appear to be very passionate about conservation. Tell your readers a bit more about that.
I am extremely passionate about conserving and protecting this perfect place. By contributing my time and energy to this goal, I find my connection to the forests ever deepening and the benefits that I reap far outweigh the energy expenditure.

What is the one take-home message you'd like to leave your readers with?
There is always magic and beauty and enchantment... just a heartbeat away; if you would but choose to see it.

CPSIA information can be obtained
at www.ICGtesting.com
Printed in the USA
BVHW04s0219160818
524708BV00012B/124/P

9 780620 716550